A Guide to
IRELAND'S RAILWAY HERITAGE

0-4-2ST "Dromad", built 1916, of the Cavan & Leitrim Railway

A Guide to
IRELAND'S RAILWAY HERITAGE

Gregg Ryan & Bernard Share

Guide du
PATRIMOINE FERROVIAIRE IRLANDAIS

Ein Führer durch
DIE VERGANGENHEIT DER IRISCHEN EISENBAHN

IARNRÓD ÉIREANN
Heritage Series n°.3
2002

Published by Iarnród Éireann,
Connolly Station,
Dublin 1

© Gregg Ryan & Bernard Share 2002

ISBN 0-9542721-0-2

Design & print origination by Conor Nolan
Printed in Ireland by ColourBooks Ltd., Dublin.

All rights reserved. No part of this publication may be copied, reproduced or transmitted in any form or by any means, without permission of the publishers.

Also in this series:

The Works. Iarnród Éireann Railway Works, Inchicore, Dublin. *Gregg Ryan*

The Station Masters. History and redevelopment of Heuston and Connolly Stations, Dublin. *Gregg Ryan & Bernard Share*

CONTENTS

Foreword	7
Introduction	10
Belturbet Railway Visitor Centre	16
Cavan & Leitrim Railway	20
Clonakilty Model Railway Village	24
Clonmacnoise & West Offaly Railway	28
Cork Station Museum	32
County Donegal Railway Restoration Society	36
Downpatrick Railway Museum	40
Foyle Valley Railway Museum	44
Fry Model Railway	48
Giant's Causeway & Bushmills Railway	52
Hell's Kitchen Railway Bar & Museum	56
Irish Railway Record Society	60
Irish Traction Group	64
Listowel & Ballybunion Railway	68
Railway Preservation Society of Ireland	72
Stradbally Railway	76
Straffan Steam Museum	80
Tralee & Dingle Railway	84
Transport Museum Society of Ireland	88
Ulster Folk & Transport Museum	92
Waterford & Suir Valley Railway	96
West Clare Railway	100
Location Map	104

ACKNOWLEDGEMENTS

The authors wish to acknowledge the co-operation and assistance of the organisations represented in this work. Their particular thanks are due to Joe Meagher, Managing Director, Joe Walsh, Inter City Manager and Ray Kelly, Marketing Manager, Iarnród Éireann; Brendan Pender and Norman McAdams of the Irish Railway Record Society; Conor Nolan and Bill Bolger of the National College of Art and Design.

FOREWORD

The history of Ireland's railways is one of the richest in the world. In every sense, the early Irish railway companies were pioneers, and the challenges they faced and overcame were equally as daunting as those which confront the leaders of technological advancement today.

Ireland's railway engineers gave the world new techniques, from the civil engineering feats of Sir John Macneill to the mechanical genius of such as Ivatt, Aspinall and Maunsell. Their brilliance, and the absolute loyalty of their colleagues at every level of railway operation, made an incalculable contribution to the growth of the commercial, economic, and social life of the whole country.

Today, we in Iarnród Éireann are the heirs of that genius and dedication. The role of the railways, neglected and under-funded for decades, is now being recognised as a vital ingredient in the future prosperity of the nation and the opening years of the new millennium are marked by unprecedented investment in the railway system. Yet, as with other national institutions, the railway of the future must not be neglectful of its past.

Iarnród Éireann is conscious of the legacy, for it is a national legacy, of which we are the custodians. All over the system we are reminded of that great past because, as is the nature of railways, the basic infrastructure changes little. Fine buildings remain in use, and the Permanent Way remains as permanent as ever. The railway of the future is committed to preserving its past and through our own heritage officer we are in regular contact with the Heritage Council and Dúchas, the heritage service.

On behalf of Inter City, I am delighted to be involved with this publication which helps underline our ongoing celebration of the past as we move forward with confidence into the future.

Joe Walsh
Manager, Inter City.
Connolly Station, Dublin 1

PREFACE

L'histoire du chemin de fer irlandais est l'une des plus riches au monde. A tous les égards, les premières compagnies ferroviaires irlandaises en furent les pionnières, et les défis auxquels elles durent faire face et qu'elles surmontèrent furent tout autant intimidants que ceux auxquels sont confrontés aujourd'hui les leaders du progrès technologique.

Nous, chez Iarnród Éireann, sommes les héritiers de ce génie et de cette consécration. Le rôle du chemin de fer, négligé et insuffisamment financé pendant des décennies, est aujourd'hui reconnu comme un ingrédient essentiel à la future prospérité de la nation et le début du millénaire a été marqué par un investissement sans précédent dans le réseau ferroviaire. Cependant, comme les autres institutions nationales, le chemin de fer du futur ne doit pas être oublieux de son passé. Au nom d'Intercity, je suis ravi de participer à cette publication qui nous permettra de perpétuer notre célébration continue du passé alors que nous transitons, avec confiance, vers l'avenir.

VORWORT

Die irische Eisenbahn hat eine der umfangreichsten Vergangenheitsgeschichten der Welt. Die frühen irischen Eisenbahnfirmen waren in jedem Sinne Pioniere. Die Aufgaben, die sie zu bewältigen hatten, waren genauso groß wie diejenigen, vor denen die heutigen Führer des technischen Fortschritts stehen.

Wir bei Iarnród Éireann sind die Erben dieses Pioniergeistes und Ehrgeizes. Die Rolle der Eisenbahnstrecken, jahrzehntelang vernachlässigt und unterfinanziert, wird nun als lebenswichtiger Bestandteil des Wohlstandes der Nation erkannt, und die Anfangsjahre des neuen Jahrtausends sind durch noch nie gesehene Investitionen in das Eisenbahnsystem gekennzeichnet. Wie bei anderen nationalen Einrichtungen auch darf, die Eisenbahn der Zukunft jedoch nicht die eigene Vergangenheit vergessen. Im Namen von Intercity freue ich mich, an dieser Veröffentlichung beteiligt zu sein, die unsere Vergangenheit feiert, während wir mit Zuversicht die Zukunft angehen.

INTRODUCTION

From their earliest days railways have always fascinated, and the heritage they have bequeathed to us through their construction and operation has left an indelible stamp on the landscape of nations throughout the world. Even where they have long since disappeared, there remain the unmistakable patterns, formations, buildings, abutments.

The enduring physical evidences of railway systems past and present serve to highlight their imprint on local communities – the memories of those who worked the lines, the people and goods they conveyed, the prosperity or otherwise which they visited upon city, town and village – and the abiding folklore and anecdotal history which enriches a society in an intangible but very real way.

In this regard Ireland, though no different from anywhere else on earth, may justifiably lay claim to a unique inheritance – including a non-standard 'standard gauge' of 5ft 3ins (1600mm) as against the European and international norm of 4ft 8 1/2ins (1470mm) and a narrow gauge 'standard gauge' of 3ft (914mm) which at one time seemed likely to compete with the wider gauge for equal route mileage and would have given the country not one, but two 'standard' standard gauges!

Ireland is unique, too, in having pioneered the first commercially practical mono-railway in the world and introduced the hydro-electric railway, to mention but a few examples of the ingenuity tested and successfully implemented in this little country. The railway has served us well, and continues to do so as it faces the brighter dawn of a new era when at last it is being recognised through investment as a transport mode which more than any other has the potential to rescue Irish society, commercially and socially, from the strangulation of road chaos and at the same time make a genuine contribution to a cleaner environment.

In 1834 the Dublin & Kingstown became not only the first railway in Ireland but arguably the first commuter railway in the world. Less than two decades later there were 840 route miles (1344 km) in operation, and by 1920, it had peaked at 3,442 miles (5507 km). Today there is less than half that, but the heritage lives on, and it is good to know that for the most part the systems and sites we visit in the following pages are accessible by Inter City or suburban rail.

Ireland's Railway Heritage is a guide to much of the railway history which surrounds us. It is a modest tribute to those whose engineering brilliance and sometimes sheer blind courage led to its creation, and to those who now strive to perpetuate it in so many ways for this and future generations to appreciate and enjoy.

Gregg W. Ryan FCIT
Heritage Officer, Iarnród Éireann,
Inchicore Railway Works, Dublin 8

INTRODUCTION

Les balisages physiques résistants des réseaux ferroviaires du passé et du présent servent à marquer leur empreinte sur les communautés locales — et notamment la mémoire de ceux qui ont travaillé sur les lignes, les voyageurs et les marchandises qu'ils ont transportés, la prospérité ou tout autre sentiment qu'ils ont connu en traversant villes et villages —, ainsi que sur le folklore et l'histoire anecdotique permanents qui enrichissent une société de manière impalpable, mais bien réelle.

A ces égards, l'Irlande n'est pas vraiment différente des autres endroits de la terre, mais peut, à juste titre, revendiquer un patrimoine unique propre à l'Irlande — tel qu'un 'chemin de fer à voie normale' non standard de 1600 mm contraire à la norme internationale et européenne de 1470 mm, et un 'chemin de fer à voie normale' de chemin de fer à voie étroite de 914 mm qui, à une époque, semblait capable de concurrencer le chemin de fer à voie plus large pour un kilométrage équivalent, et aurait donné au pays non pas un, mais deux chemins de fer 'standards' à voie normale !

L'Irlande est unique, également, dans sa construction du premier monorail commercialisé dans le monde, bien qu'il soit à vapeur, et fut pionnière dans le lancement du chemin de fer hydroélectrique, pour ne mentionner que quelques exemples de l'ingéniosité testée et mise en œuvre de façon magistrale dans ce petit pays. Le chemin de fer nous a bien servi, et continue de le faire alors qu'il se voit contraint de faire face à l'aube la plus brillante d'une nouvelle ère où il est enfin reconnu, grâce aux investissements réalisés, comme un moyen de transport qui, plus que tous les autres, possède le potentiel de sauver la société irlandaise, sur le plan commercial et social, de l'asphyxie du chaos des routes et par la même occasion, d'apporter une véritable contribution à un environnement plus propre.

Le patrimoine ferroviaire irlandais est un guide retraçant l'histoire du chemin de fer qui nous entoure. Il rend hommage à ceux dont l'intelligence scientifique de l'ingénierie et parfois le courage aveugle absolu sont à l'origine de sa création, ainsi qu'à ceux qui luttent aujourd'hui pour perpétuer son existence de diverses manières pour la joie et l'appréciation des générations actuelles et à venir.

EINLEITUNG

Die zeitbeständigen Zeugen der vergangenen und heutigen Eisenbahnsysteme haben einen bleibenden Einfluss auf die örtliche Gemeinschaft — da sind Erinnerungen an diejenigen, die an den Strecken gearbeitet haben, an die Leute und Waren, die damit transportiert wurden, den Wohlstand, den sie den Städten, Dörfern und Gemeinden gebracht haben oder auch nicht — und dann noch die damit zusammenhängende Folklore und die Geschichten, die die Gesellschaft in unwiderruflicher aber sehr realer Weise bereichern.

In dieser Beziehung ist Irland nicht anderes als andere Länder der Welt, kann aber vielleicht eine einzigartige Vergangenheit vorweisen, die nur Irland zustandebringen kann — wie eine nicht-standardmäßiges Standardspurweite von 1600mm im Vergleich zu der europäischen und internationalen Norm von 1470mm, und einer Standard-Schmalspur von 914mm, die einstmals der breiteren Spur in Bezug auf Schienenkilometer fast den Rang abgelaufen hätte, so dass das Land nicht nur eine, sondern zwei „Standard"-Spurweiten gehabt hätte.

Irland ist auch das einzige Land, das die erste kommerziell einsetzbare Einschienenbahn entwickelt hat, und zwar mit Dampfantrieb, und außerdem die Hydro-elektrische Einsenbahn eingeführt hat, um nur ein paar Beispiele des in diesem kleinen Land getesteten und erfolgreich umgesetzten Erfindungsreichtums zu nennen. Die Eisenbahn hat und gut gedient und dient uns auch weiterhin, während wir einer besseren Zukunft entgegen gehen, in der sie in Form von Investitionen als ein Transportmittel anerkannt wird, das mehr als jedes andere das Potential hat, die irische Gesellschaft in kommerzieller und sozialer Hinsicht vom Würgegriff des Verkehrschaos zu retten und gleichzeitig einen Beitrag zu einer sauberen Umwelt zu leisten.

Die Vergangenheit der irischen Eisenbahn ist ein Führer durch unsere Eisenbahnvergangenheit Es ist ein Dank an diejenigen, die durch technische Brillanz und manchesmal reinen Mut zu der Entstehung beigetragen haben und diejenigen, die nun diese Tradition auf so viele verschiedene Weisen zum Wohle dieser und zukünftiger Generationen weiterzuführen versuchen.

The dismantled components of locomotive no. 131 of the former Great Northern Railway at the Inchicore works of Iarnród Éireann. It is planned to reassemble and restore it to full working order.

Les pièces démontées de la locomotive n°131 de l'ancien chemin de fer de Great Northern à l'usine d'Inchicore d'Iarnród Éireann. Son remontage et sa remise en état intégrale sont prévus.

Die zerlegten Bauteile von Lokomotive Nr. 131 der früheren Great Northern Railway in dem Inchicore-Werken von Iarnród Éireann. Es ist beabsichtigt, diese wieder zusammenzusetzen und die Lok wieder in einen betriebsbereiten Zustand zu versetzen.

BELTURBET RAILWAY VISITOR CENTRE

At the end of a short (7.2km) branch from Ballyhaise on the line from Clones to Cavan, Belturbet station was opened in 1885. It was both a terminus and a through station, since it was here that the Dundalk & Enniskillen Railway and its successor, the Great Northern, met head-on, so to speak, with the narrow-gauge Cavan & Leitrim (see pps. 20—23). The station layout provided platforms and engine sheds for both gauges and a tranship shed, served by both companies, in which goods were transferred from one to the other. Arigna coal was, throughout the history of the station, moved arduously from the C&L to the GNR by local men with shovels.

The partition of Ireland in 1922 seriously affected traffic on both the C&L and the Great Northern in this border area, and though the lines struggled on through and after World War II, the closure of much of the rail network in Northern Ireland in the 1950s spelt the end for both companies, which ceased operations within a day of each other on 31 March/1 April 1959.

Many of the buildings of both railways are still on site, including the main GNR station, the stationmaster's house, the GNR goods store and engine shed, the tranship shed and the water tower. The fine station building was the only one on the GNR system to be built of cut stone, quarried locally. Its wall dividing the public area from the waiting room has been removed to create a large reception hall, but otherwise it remains largely as it was built, having been painstakingly and authentically restored after 40 years of dereliction.

Belturbet Community Development Association bought the station site in 1995 and commenced the demanding task of restoration and the creation of a Centre of major interest for railway historians and enthusiasts. It now houses memorabilia including artefacts and documents and a collection of rolling stock in course of restoration. Conference and meeting facilities are located in the restored goods store and other elements of the project, including eight self-catering apartments, are being completed as funds become available.

Location: Railway Road, Belturbet, Co. Cavan
Access: No Intercity rail connection. Bus Éireann service from Dublin.
Operation: 09.30—17.00 Mon.—Fri. all year. 10.00—17.00 weekends and national holidays May — Sept.
Telephone: 00353—49—9522074 **Fax**: 00353—49—9522581
Website: www.belturbet-station.com **Email**: info@belturbet-station.com

Belturbet Station: GNR standard gauge (R); Cavan & Leitrim narrow gauge (L). *(W.A. Camwell, IRRS collection)*

Située sur un court embranchement (7,2 km) de Ballyhaise sur la ligne Clones — Cavan, la gare de chemin de fer de Belturbet fut ouverte en 1885. Elle servait tant de terminus que de gare de passage jusqu'à ce que les chemins de fer Dundalk & Enniskillen et son successeur, le Great Northern, se confrontent, pour ainsi dire, au chemin de fer à voie étroite Cavan & Leitrim (Cf. pps. 20—23). L'aménagement de la gare fournissait des plates-formes et des dépôts de locomotives servant aux deux écartements de voie ainsi qu'une halle de transbordement, utilisée par les deux compagnies, au sein de laquelle les marchandises étaient transférées d'une compagnie à l'autre.

La division de l'Irlande en 1922 affecta sérieusement le trafic du C&L et du Great Northern dans cette zone limitrophe, et bien que les lignes survécurent pendant et après la Seconde guerre mondiale, la fermeture de la majeure partie du réseau ferroviaire de l'Irlande du Nord dans les années 50 précipita la chute des deux compagnies, qui cessèrent leurs opérations un jour après l'autre, le 31 mars et le 1er avril 1959.

De nombreux bâtiments des deux gares se trouvent encore aujourd'hui sur le site. Le magnifique bâtiment de gare fut le seul du réseau GNR à avoir été construit en pierre de taille, dont l'exploitation fut locale. Son mur séparant la zone réservée au public de la salle d'attente fut détruit pour construire un hall de réception plus vaste, mais sinon, elle demeura pratiquement similaire à sa forme d'origine, ayant subi une rénovation dans le plus grand soin et authenticité au bout de 40 ans d'abandon. Le centre d'accueil, qui constitue un intérêt majeur pour les historiens et les passionnés du chemin de fer, abrite aujourd'hui des souvenirs tels que divers objets et documents ainsi qu'une collection de parcs à wagons en cours de restauration. Des locaux aménagés pour l'organisation de conférences et de réunions, sont situés dans l'entrepôt de marchandises restauré et huit chambres meublées ont été mises à la disposition de ceux qui souhaitent prolonger leur séjour dans une région du pays, belle et encore intacte.

Am Ende eines kurzen Abzweigs (7,2 km) von Ballyhaise auf der Strecke von Clones nach Cavan wurde 1885 der Bahnhof von Belturbet eröffnet. Er war sowohl Endstation als auch Durchgangsbahnhof, da sich hier die Dundalk & Enniskillen Railway und ihr Vorgänger, die Great Northern, sozusagen Kopf an Kopf mit der Schmalspurbahn Kevin & Leitrim Railway trafen (siehe Seiten 20—23). Dieser Bahnhof hatte Plattformen und Lokomotivschuppen für beide Spurweiten, und außerdem einen Umladeschuppen, der von beiden Firmen genutzt wurde und in dem die Waren von einer Bahn auf die andere umgeladen wurden.

Die Teilung Irlands im Jahre 1922 hatte schwerwiegende Auswirkungen auf den Verkehr sowohl von C&L als auch der Great Northern in diesem Grenzgebiet, und obwohl beide Gesellschaften den zweiten Weltkrieg und die Nachkriegszeit überlebten, bedeutete die Stilllegung eines großen Teils des Schienennetzwerks in Nordirland in den 50er Jahren das Aus für beide Firmen, die beide innerhalb von 2 Tagen, am 31. Mai und am 1. April 1959, den Betrieb einstellten.

Viele der Gebäude beider Einsenbahngesellschaften stehen heute noch. Das schöne Bahnhofsgebäude war das einzige Gebäude des GNR-Systems. das aus behauenen Steinen gebaut wurde, die aus einem örtlichen Steinbruch stammten. Die Wände, die den der Öffentlichkeit zugänglichen Bereich von dem Warteraum trennten, wurden entfernt, um eine große Empfangshalle zu schaffen, ansonsten ist der Bahnhof im wesentlichen so erhalten, wie er gebaut wurde, nachdem er sorgfältig und authentisch nach 40 Jahren der Vernachlässigung restauriert wurde. Das Zentrum, von großem Interesse für Eisenbahnhistoriker und —enthusiasten, beherbergt nun Erinnerungsstücke, u. a. Teile, Dokumente und eine Sammlung Waggons, die gerade restauriert werden. Konferenz- und Versammlungsräume befinden sich in dem restaurierten Warenlager, und es gibt auf dem Gelände acht Selbstversorger-Appartments für diejenigen, die sich länger in dieser wunderschönen und unverschandelten Gegend aufhalten möchten.

CAVAN & LEITRIM RAILWAY

The original Cavan & Leitrim Railway operated its first train – a pig special – on 6 September 1887, and its last, consisting of all available coaches and vans packed to overflowing, on the night of 31 March 1959. Serving a remote and rural part of the country with a scattered population and, apart from the coal mines of Arigna, no significant industries, it was never prosperous nor profitable. In its latter days it struggled with a motley collection of locomotives bequeathed to it from the once extensive system of narrow-gauge lines (including the Tralee & Dingle Railway, see pps. 84–87).

Yet the C&L within its limitations served its small community well, not only linking isolated villages and small towns with a vital transport facility in the days when few had any alternative but providing a means of travelling further afield, since it connected at both termini with the standard gauge network. The sole branch, from Ballinamore to the Arigna mines, latterly provided the main revenue for the undertaking, particularly during the period of World War II (known in neutral Ireland as 'The Emergency'.

In the early 1900s members of the Narrow Gauge Trust began to develop the terminus at Dromod as a site for museum material they had collected, and out of this grew a determination to restore a section of the C&R as a working railway. Much of the trackbed remained in situ, as did many of the buildings including the station and water tower at Dromod. An 800m section of the line, together with workshops, sidings and static exhibits, has now been reopened and it is planned to extend this as far as Mohill (8 kms) where the fine station building has already been reinstated.

The reborn C&L operates both steam and diesel services for visitors, the former powered by a rebuilt 0-4-2 Kerr Stuart locomotive named Dromad with a second engine in course of being restored. There is a great deal more of railway, general transport and industrial archaeological interest at the site, including diesel locomotives and equipment from the extensive Bord na

Móna system (see pps. 28—31).

Location: Station Road, Dromod, Co. Leitrim
Access: Intercity rail from Dublin, Sligo and intermediate points.
Operation: Weekends May—October. 'Santa Specials' at Christmas. Special groups by arrangement. Visitors welcome 7 days (10.30—18.00).
Telephone/Fax: 00—353—078 38599

Mixed train at Mohill *(W.A. Camwell, IRRS collection)*

Le chemin de fer Cavan & Leitrim d'origine mit en service son premier train — spécialement destiné au transport des porcs — le 6 septembre 1887, et son dernier, composé de toutes les voitures à couloir central et de tous les wagons de queue disponibles à profusion, dans la nuit du 31 mars 1959. Desservant une partie rurale reculée du pays habitée par une population éparpillée, et où, excepté les mines de charbon locales d'Arigna, aucune industrie majeure n'y était implantée, le réseau ferroviaire ne se révéla jamais ni prospère ni rentable. Dans ses derniers jours, il fonctionnait péniblement avec une collection hétéroclite de locomotives qui lui avait été léguée par le réseau autrefois important des lignes à voie étroite (y compris celui de Tralee & Dingle Railway, cf. pps. 84—87).

Après sa renaissance, C&R utilise des machines à vapeur et Diesel pour accomplir ses services à l'attention des visiteurs, ses anciennes machines fonctionnant à l'aide d'une locomotive reconstruite de Kerr Stuart 0-2-1 appelée Dromad possédant un second moteur en cours de restauration. Beaucoup de choses sur le chemin de fer, le transport en général et l'intérêt archéologique industriel valent la peine d'être vues sur ce site, y compris des locomotives Diesel et du matériel appartenant au vaste réseau de Bord na Móna (Cf. pps. 24—27).

Kerr Stuart No.1 "Dromad" at Dromod Station (Opposite)

Die ursprüngliche Cavan & Leitrim Railway fuhr ihren ersten Zug – einen Schweinetransport – am 6. September 1887 und ihren letzten mit allen zur Verfügung stehenden Waggons, die zum Bersten voll waren, am Abend des 31. März 1959. Da diese Strecke ein entlegenes und ländliches Gebiet mit geringer Bevölkerungsdichte und, mit Ausnahme der Zechen von Arigna, ohne Industrie versorgte, war sie nie ertragreich oder gewinnbringend. In den späteren Tagen litt sie unter einer buntgemischten Sammlung von Lokomotiven, die sie von dem einst umfangreichen Netz der Schmalspurbahnen geerbt hatte (einschl. Trallee & Dingle Railway, siehe Seiten 84–87).

Die neugeborene C&R betreibt für ihre Besucher sowohl Dampf- als auch Diesellokomotiven, wobei erstere von einer restaurierten 0-2-1 Kerr Stuart Lokomotive mit Namen Dromad angetrieben wird. Eine zweite Lokomotive wird gerade restauriert. Es gibt viele andere interessante Dinge in Bezug auf Einsenbahn, Transport im allgemeinen und industrielle Archäologie, u. a. Diesellokomotiven und Ausrüstungen des umfangreichen Bord na Móna Systems (siehe Seiten 24–27).

CLONAKILTY MODEL RAILWAY VILLAGE

Clonakilty was the terminus of a branch on the Cork, Bandon and South Coast Railway, an extensive system which served West Cork faithfully from 1851 until 1961. Its Cork terminus at Albert Quay was connected to the rest of the national railway network by a street tramway to the main Dublin line at Glanmire Road station, and one of the most fascinating scenes for railway enthusiasts, and occasionally the general public, was that of a steam locomotive vying with road traffic as it hauled rolling stock on transfer between the two railheads.

The backbone of the CB&SCR was the route from Albert Quay to the remote fishing village of Baltimore on the Atlantic coast; but branches ran to Courtmacsherry, Kinsale, Bantry and of course, Clonakilty, comprising in all a system of some 160 km which ran through some spectacular scenery and featured major engineering works of note including the Chetwynd Viaduct. The line became something of a Mecca for the railway enthusiasts of the 1950s with its distinctive locomotives such as the 'Bandon tanks' and boasted an unfailingly friendly staff and local population.

As part of the rationalisation of the railway system nationally, the railways of West Cork had passed to the control of Córas Iompair Éireann (CIÉ) the State transportation company. In common with branch lines to remote and sparsely populated areas elsewhere, competition from the more flexible road motor car and lorry eroded the line's patronage and it was closed throughout in April 1961. Many years later, however, the railways of the county were to receive a posthumous tribute – but a spectacular and abiding one – in the shape of the West Cork Model Railway Village.

When recession hit the West Cork town in the mid-1980s the local people decided to help themselves by developing their considerable tourism assets. The result was the miniature railway village which not only provides a faithful replica of the former CB&SCR but also the local architecture and folklore of the 1940s. Models are to scale and include locomotives, goods and passenger rolling stock built by former CIÉ railway engineer Tommy Tighe who also restored and augmented the Fry Model Railway at Malahide Castle (See pps 48–51). The collection is enhanced by the re-creation in miniature of sections of the Bandon, Dunmanway and Kinsale lines.

Location: The Station, Inchydoney Road, Clonakilty, Co. Cork.
Access: Inter City rail to Cork served from Dublin and intermediate points. Local transport from Cork city
Operation: February—October daily 11.00—17.00; Summer 10.00—18.00
Telephone: 00—353—23 33224 **Fax**: 00—353—23 34843
Email: modelvillage@eircom.net
Website: www.clonakilty.ie

Clonakilty Junction in steam days. Branch line engine on R.
(W.A. Camwell, IRRS collection)

Clonakilty fut le terminus d'un embranchement situé sur le chemin de fer de Cork, Bandon et de South Coast, un vaste réseau ayant desservi fidèlement West Cork de 1851 à 1961. Son terminus de Cork, situé à Albert Quay, était relié au reste du réseau ferroviaire national par un tramway urbain provenant de la ligne principale de la gare de Glanmire Road à Dublin, et l'un des lieux les plus fascinants aux yeux des passionnés du chemin de fer, et occasionnellement du grand public, fut celui d'une locomotive à vapeur rivalisant avec le trafic routier alors qu'il transportait des parcs à wagons entre la tête et la queue de la ligne.

En tant qu'étape de la rationalisation du réseau ferroviaire à l'échelle nationale, les chemins de fer de West Cork passèrent le contrôle de CIÉ, la compagnie de transport de l'état. Comme pour les embranchements reliés aux régions reculées et habitées par une population éparse, la concurrence de l'automobile et du camion à moteur plus flexible usa la fréquentation de la ligne, et celle-ci fut fermée au cours du mois d'avril 1961. De nombreuses années plus tard, cependant, les chemins de fer du comté reçurent un hommage posthume – Et, un hommage spectaculaire et permanent – sous la forme du village miniature du chemin de fer de West Cork.

Lorsque la récession frappa la ville de West Cork au milieu des années 80, les habitants locaux décidèrent de s'en sortir en développant leurs considérables trésors culturels. Le résultat fut le village miniature du chemin de fer qui, non seulement offrait une réplique fidèle de l'ancien CB&SCR, mais également de l'architecture et du folklore locaux des années 40. Les modèles sont à l'échelle et parmi eux figurent des locomotives, un parc à wagons de marchandises et de voyageurs construit par l'ancien ingénieur des chemins de fer de CIÉ, Tommy Tighe, qui entreprit également la restauration et l'agrandissement du modèle de chemin de fer de Fry au château de Malahide (Cf. pps 48–51).

Clonakilty war der Endbahnhof einer Zweigstrecke von Cork über Bandon zur Südküste, einem umfangreichen System, das West Cork von 1851 bis 1961 versorgte. Der Bahnhof in Cork am Alberts Quay war mit dem Rest des nationalen Steckensystems über eine Straßenbahn zum Bahnhof in der Glanmire Road an der Strecke nach Dublin verbunden. Eins der für Eisenbahnenthusiasten und gelegentlich auch für die Öffentlichkeit faszinierensten Ereignisse war der Anblick einer mit dem Straßenverkehr konkurrierenden Lokomotive, die ihre Waggons von einem zum anderen Bahnhof zog.

Als Teil der Rationalisierung des nationalen Einsenbahnsystems wurde das Einsenbahnsystem in West Cork CIÉ unterstellt, der staatlichen Transportgesellschaft. So wie anderswo auch, bekamen die Zweigstrecken zu allen entlegenen und dünn besiedelten Gebieten die Konkurrenz der flexibleren Autos und Lkws zu spüren. Die Strecke verlor an Bedeutung und wurde im April 1961 ganz stillgelegt. Viele Jahre später wurden die Eisenbahnstrecken der Grafschaft im nachhinein geehrt – spektakulär und nachhaltig – in Form der „West Cork Model Railway Village".

In der Mitte der 80er Jahre, als diese Stadt in West Cork von der Rezession erfasst wurde, entschieden die Ortsansässigen, sich durch die Entwicklung der bedeutenden Tourismusbranche selbst zu helfen. Das Ergebnis war das Miniatur-Eisenbahndorf, das nicht nur eine naturgetreue Nachbildung der früheren CB&SCR ist sondern auch die örtliche Architektur und Folklore wiederspiegelt. Die Modelle sind maßstabsgetreu und umfassen Lokomotiven, Güter- und Personenwagen, gebaut von dem früheren CIÉ-Eisenbahningenieur Tommy Tighe, der auch die „Fry Model Railway" am Malahide Castle restaurierte und aufbaute. (siehe Seiten 48—51)

CLONMACNOISE & WEST OFFALY RAILWAY

Those who thought the commercial narrow gauge railways of Ireland had come to the end of the line by 1960 may be surprised to learn that Bord na Móna, the State peat authority, operates some 800 km of 3ft gauge railway for transporting milled and sod peat to power stations for electricity generation and for processing into briquettes for domestic and industrial use and for horticultural applications.

Until the Clonmacnoise and West Offaly Railway was born, none of this extensive system, sections of which are lifted and relaid elsewhere as harvesting work on the bogs progresses, has been open to the general public. Three steam locomotives, provided for the system in 1949 by Andrew Barclay, were the only ones ever to operate on the Bord na Móna lines and their working lives were short-lived. Two are now on private systems at Stradbally (see pps 76–79) and at Bushmills (See pps 52–55) while the third now operates in the United Kingdom.

The mainstays of the current locomotive fleet are Simplex, Deutz and Wagonmaster, and it is one of the latter which hauls the Clonmacnoise and West Offaly train, made up of specially built passenger coaches with a public address system providing a commentary by a knowledgeable tour guide. The idea came from two members of the Bord na Móna staff – Pat Dooley and Paddy Byrne – who saw an opportunity to introduce visitors to the topography, archaeology and wild life of one of Ireland's greatest natural resources. Since its inception in 1993 has been a great success.

The 8 km trip is of an hour's duration, across some of the most unusual terrain to be found anywhere in Europe – bogs which have taken thousands of years to 'grow' and which support unique wildlife and plant life while from time to time yielding up fascinating archaeological treasures. On the journey you will probably cross one of the heavily laden peat trains on its journey to nearby Shannonbridge power station, an example of the modern peat industry at work.

Location: Blackwater Works (Uisce Dubh), near Shannonbridge, Co. Offaly
Access: Inter City rail to Athlone, served from Dublin and intermediate points. Local transport from Athlone.
Operation: Every hour on the hour from 10.00—17.00
Telephone: 0905—74114/74172 **Fax:** 0905—74210
Email: bograil@bnm.ie
Website: www.bnm.ie

The Bog Tour Train

Bord na Móna Railcar C47, used for transporting staff and equipment. Now on the Cavan & Leitrim Railway.

Ceux qui pensaient que les chemins de fer marchands à voie étroite irlandais avaient disparu dans les années 60 pourraient être surpris s'apprendre que Bord na Móna, les autorités d'état en charge de la tourbe, font fonctionner quelques 800 km de chemin de fer à voie étroite (914mm), destinés au transport de tourbe broyée et de tourbe mottière pour alimenter les stations de génération d'électricité et pour la transformation en briquettes pour un usage domestique et industriel, ainsi que pour les applications dans l'horticulture. Une partie de ce vaste réseau est aujourd'hui ouverte au grand public.

Les modèles principaux du parc actuel de locomotives Diesel sont Simplex, Deutz et Wagonmaster, et c'est l'une de ces derniers qui tira le train de Clonmacnoise et de West Offaly, composé de voitures à voyageurs construites tout spécialement avec un système de diffusion sonore publique, permettant à un guide bien informé de communiquer aux passager des informations sur les excursions. L'idée naquit dans l'esprit de deux membres du personnel de Bord na Móna qui virent là une occasion de présenter aux visiteurs la topographie, l'archéologie et la faune et la flore de l'une des ressources naturelles les plus importantes d'Irlande. Depuis son lancement en 1993, cela se révèle être une grande réussite.

Le parcours de 8 km d'une durée d'une heure à travers certains des paysages les plus inhabituels d'Europe – des marécages ayant mis des milliers d'années à 'pousser' et abritant une faune, une flore et des végétaux uniques alors que, de temps à autre, ils produisent des trésors archéologiques fascinants. Sur le trajet, vous croiserez probablement l'un des trains lourdement chargés de tourbe au cours de son voyage en direction de la centrale électrique la plus proche de Shannonbridge, un modèle d'industrie moderne de la tourbe en fonctionnement.

Diejenigen, die gedacht haben, dass die kommerzielle Schmalspurbahn bis 1960 verschwunden war, werden wohl erstaunt sein zu erfahren, dass Bord na Móna, die staatliche Torfgesellschaft, 800 km der Eisenbahn mit der 914mm-Spur zum Transport des gemahlenen Torfs und der Torfsoden zu den Kraftwerken zur Stromerzeugung und zur Verarbeitung zu Briketts zur privaten und industriellen Verwendung und zum Gartenbau betreibt. Teil dieses umfangreichen Systems ist nun der Öffentlichkeit zugänglich.

Die Flotte der Diesellokomotiven besteht heute zum größten Teil aus Simplex-, Deutz- und Wagonmaster-Lokomotiven- Letztere zieht den Clonmacnoise and West Offaly-Zug, der aus speziell gebauten Personenwagen besteht, die mit einem Durchsagesystem ausgestattet sind, mit dem ein gut informierter Führer die Fahrt kommentiert. Die Idee stammt von zwei Bord na Móna Mitarbeitern, die die Möglichkeit sahen, Besuchern die Topographie, Archäologie und die Tierwelt eines der größten Naturschätze Irlands vorzustellen. Seit seiner Einführung im Jahre 1993 ist dieses Angebot ein großer Erfolg.

Die 8 km Fahrt dauert eine Stunde und führt durch eins der ungewöhnlichsten Gegenden Europas – Moore, die über Tausende von Jahren entstanden sind und eine ungewöhnliche Tier- und Pflanzenwelt beherbergen und ab und zu faszinierende archäologische Schätze preisgeben. Auf der Fahrt kreuzen Sie wahrscheinlich einen der schwer beladenen Torfzüge auf seiner Fahrt zu dem nahegelegenen Shannonbridge-Stromkraftwerk – ein Beispiel der modernen Torfindustrie im Einsatz.

CORK STATION MUSEUM

The Museum has its roots in the formation of a benevolent fund, led by Iarnród Éireann inspectors Billy Arnold of North Esk Depot and Tom Fenlon of Penrose Quay. Assisted by a dedicated committee, they brought together a magnificent collection of photographs, working models, uniforms and artefacts. Until a few years ago the display was beyond the reach of the public because it was housed in North Esk Freight depot. However, in 1999 the former International Travel Office at Kent Station became available and was quickly transformed into the present Museum, opened in the same year as part of the celebrations marking the arrival of the railway to Cork a century and a half before.

Some of the exhibits are very rare and date back well into the 19th century. Those on view represent only a fraction of the material at the Museum's disposal, enabling the collection to be changed at intervals.

In Millennium year 2000 the Cork curators' efforts were recognised officially when they won the Iarnród Éireann Heritage Award, a perpetual trophy in the form of a crystal glass replica of the famous Dublin-Cork express engine "Maedhbh" created by Waterford Crystal craftsman Ken McEvoy.

The Cork Museum is staffed by pensioners and is opened on request.

Location: Kent Station, Cork
Access: Inter City rail to Cork from Dublin and intermediate points
Operation: Daily 10.00—14.00 on request. *Special groups by arrangement.*
Telephone: 00—353—21 504777

Note: While in Kent Station do not miss the static exhibit in the booking hall. The oldest preserved locomotive in Ireland, Bury 2-2-2 No. 36 of the former Great Southern & Western Railway was built in 1847 and ran 576,000 km. on passenger services before its withdrawal.

Lifting bridge formerly carrying a tramway link between Cork Glanmire and Albert Quay stations. See pps. 24—27

The oldest preserved locomotive in Ireland, in Cork Glanmire Station.

Le musée tire ses origines de la création d'une caisse de bienfaisance dirigée par les contrôleurs d'Iarnród Éireann, Billy Arnold du dépôt de North Esk et Tom Fenlon de Penrose Quay. Aidés par un comité spécialisé, ils ont rassemblé ensemble une magnifique collection de photos, de trains miniatures en fonctionnement, d'uniformes et d'objets divers. Jusqu'à ces quelques dernières années, la collection était restée trop éloignée du public car elle était abritée dans le dépôt de fret. Néanmoins, en 1999, les locaux de l'ancien International Travel Office (Agence de voyages internationale) situé à la gare de Kent furent disponibles et se transformèrent rapidement pour abriter le musée actuel, qui ouvrit la même année et faisait partie intégrante des festivités marquant l'arrivée du chemin de fer à Cork un siècle et demi plus tôt.

Certaines pièces exposées sont très rares et datent probablement du 19ème siècle. Ces modèles représentent seulement une infime portion du matériel possédé par le musée, ce qui permet à la collection de se renouveler régulièrement.

En l'an 2000 marquée par l'arrivée du nouveau millénaire, les efforts des conservateurs de Cork furent officiellement reconnus lorsqu'ils remportèrent le prix Iarnród Éireann Heritage Award, un trophée éternel représentant une réplique en cristal de la célèbre locomotive de l'express Dublin-Cork « Maedhbh », créé par l'artisan Ken McEvoy pour Waterford Crystal.

Le personnel du musée de Cork est composé de retraités et est ouvert sur demande.

Remarque Pendant que vous vous trouvez à la gare de Kent, ne manquez pas l'exposition permanente se déroulant dans la salle des billets. La locomotive préservée la plus ancienne d'Irlande, Bury 1-1-1 N° 36 de l'ancien chemin de fer de Great Southern & Western fut construite en 1847 et parcourut 576 000 km de services voyageurs avant d'être supprimée.

Das Museum hat seine Wurzeln in einem Wohltätigkeitsfund, der von den Iarnród Éireann-Inspektoren Billy Arnold vom North Esk Depot und Tom Fenlon vom Penrose Quay geleitet wurde. Unterstützt von einem fleißigen Komitee haben sie eine wunderbare Sammlung von Fotos, funktionsfähigen Modellen, Uniformen und Gegenständen zusammengetragen. Bis vor einigen Jahren war die Sammlung der Öffentlichkeit nicht zugänglich, da diese im North Esk Frachtdepot untergebracht war. Im Jahre 1999 wurde jedoch das frühere International Travel Office im Kent Station frei. Es wurde schnell zu dem heutigen Museum umgebaut, das noch im gleichen Jahr als Teil der Festlichkeiten zur Erinnerung an die Ankunft der Eisenbahn in Cork vor anderthalb Jahrhunderten eröffnet wurde.

Einige der Ausstellungsstücke sind sehr selten und stammen aus dem 19. Jahrhundert. Die ausgestellten Stücke sind nur einen Teil der Sammlung des Museums, so dass sie Ausstellung von zeit zu Zeit geändert werden kann.

Im Milleniumsjahr 2000 wurden die Bemühungen der Kuratoren aus Cork offiziell gewürdigt, als sie den Iarnród Éireann Heritage Award gewannen, eine Trophäe in Form einer Kristallnachbildung der berühmten Dublin-Cork-Express-Lokomotive "Maedhbh", die von dem Kunsthandwerker Ken McEvoy von Waterford Crystal hergestellt wurde.

Das Personal im Museum in Cork besteht aus Pensionären und wird auf Anfrage geöffnet.

Anmerkung: Verpassen Sie bei Ihrem Aufenthalt in der Kent Station nicht das Dauerdisplay in der Schalterhalle. Die älteste erhaltene Lokomotive in Irlands, Bury 1-1-1 No. 36 der früheren Great Southern & Western Railway, wurde 1847 gebaut und ist 576.000 km im Personenverkehr gelaufen, bevor sie stillgelegt wurde.

COUNTY DONEGAL RAILWAY RESTORATION SOCIETY

One of the most extensive narrow gauge systems in Ireland or Britain, the County Donegal in its heyday operated over almost 200 route km in the remote North West. The system had its origins in the Finn Valley Railway which was opened as a 5ft 3in gauge line in 1863 and later rebuilt to the Irish 'standard' narrow-gauge of 914mm. The West Donegal Railway, built between 1882-89, was amalgamated with Finn Valley to form the Donegal Railway and the new entity was subsequently joined by the Strabane & Letterkenny Railway, opened in 1909. Control of the whole undertaking was vested in the County Donegal Railways Joint Committee, administered by the Great Northern Railway of Ireland and the Midland Railway of England.

It was on the County Donegal that the GNR(I)'s early pioneering of diesel railcars was seen to most effect, providing the mainstay for the passenger services on the system from the early 1930s with quaint, very bus-like articulated vehicles. These allowed for request stops at the many road crossings and added to the flexibility of a service which nevertheless finally closed on 31 December 1959, having struggled against road competition for many years,

The CDR also possessed a fine stock of steam locomotives, some of which have been preserved after having languished in the open air, exposed to the elements and vandals for more than three decades. Several of these impressive machines are now under the protection of preservation bodies, and one of them, Drumboe, may be seen at the entrance to the station yard at the Donegal Town, headquarters of the County Donegal Railway Restoration Society.

This heritage centre occupies most of the former station building and the visitor is guided through the history of railways in Donegal with models, photographs, video displays, artefacts and documents. There is also a working model railway and a bookshop stocking memorabilia of this once great system. Plans are well in hand to relay about 2 km of the line from the station yard to a former gatehouse.

Location: Old Railway Station, Tyrconnell Street, Donegal Town
Access: Inter City rail to Sligo, bus to Donegal.
Operation: June—September, Monday—Saturday 09:00—17:30hrs, Sundays 14:00—17:00hrs.
October—May, Monday—Friday 10:00—17:00hrs, closed Saturday and Sunday.
Telephone/Fax: 00—353—73 22655

Old Railway Station, Donegal Town.

L'un des réseaux à voie étroite les plus importants d'Irlande ou de Grande-Bretagne, celui du comté de Donegal, desservait, à son heure de gloire, pratiquement 200 km d'itinéraire dans la région reculée du Nord-Ouest. Le réseau tire ses origines du chemin de fer de Finn Valley qui fut ouvert sous la forme d'une ligne à voie avec écartement de 1600mm en 1863 et fut reconstruite plus tard selon la 'norme' irlandaise de chemin de fer à voie étroite de 914 mm. Ce fut dans le comté de Donegal que la toute première apparition des autorails Diesel eut le plus grand impact, jouant le rôle de soutien principal des services voyageurs du réseau au début des années 30, grâce à des véhicules articulés d'une grande originalité, ressemblant à des bus. Ceux-ci ajoutèrent à la flexibilité d'un service qui, néanmoins, finit par fermer le 31 décembre 1959, après une lutte sans merci pendant de nombreuses années, contre la concurrence de la route,

Le CDR possédait également un stock de superbes locomotives, parmi lesquelles certaines furent préservées. Plusieurs de ces machines impressionnantes sont aujourd'hui sous la protection d'organismes de préservation, et l'un d'eux, le Drumboe, peut être visité à l'entrée du hall de gare de la ville de Donegal, le siège de l'association de restauration du chemin de fer du comté de Donegal. Ce centre du patrimoine occupe la majorité de l'ancien bâtiment de gare et guide le visiteur à travers l'histoire du chemin de fer à Donegal à l'aide de modèles, de photographies, de diffusions vidéo, d'objets et de documents. Un chemin de fer miniature en fonctionnement ainsi qu'une librairie présentant des souvenirs de ce réseau autrefois important, s'y trouvent également. Les plans sont bien partis pour relayer environ 2 km de la ligne depuis le hall de gare à destination d'un ancien poste de garde.

Eins der größten Schmalspursysteme in Irland und Großbritannien, die County Donegal, betrieb zur ihrer Blütezeit fast 200 km Schienenstrecke im entlegenen Nordwesten. Der Ursprung des Systems war die Finn Valley Railway, die als Bahn mit einer Spur von 1600mm im Jahre 1863 eröffnet wurde und später auf den irischen Schmalspurstandard von 914mm umgebaut wurde. Auf der County Donegal fand die eigentliche Einführung der Dieseltriebwagen statt, die den Hauptteil der Passagierbeförderung auf dieser Strecke ab den 30er Jahren übernahmen. Die Wagen hatten viel Ähnlichkeit mit den alten Gelenkbussen. Diese erhöhten die Flexibilität des Dienstes, der trotzdem am 31. Dezember 1959 nach einem mehrjährigen Kampf gegen den Wettbewerb auf der Straße eingestellt wurde.

Die CDR besaß außerdem eine feine Sammlung an Dampflokomotiven, von denen einige erhalten geblieben sind. Mehrere dieser beeindruckenden Maschinen stehen nun unter dem Schutz von Schutzorganisationen. Eine von diesen, die Drumboe, kann am Eingang des Bahnhofs in der Stadt Donegal besichtigt werden, dem Hauptquartier der County Donegal Railway Restoration Society. Dieses Museum erstreckt sich über den Großteil des früheren Bahnhofsgebäudes, und der Besucher wird mit Modellen, Fotos, Videos, Displays, Originalstücken und Dokumenten durch die Vergangenheit der Eisanbahnen in Donegal geführt. Hier befindet sich auch eine betriebsfähige Modelleisenbahn und ein Buchgeschäft, in dem Erinnerungsstücke an dieses einstmals große System zu finden sind. Es bestehen Pläne, etwa 2 km Schiene von dem Bahnhof zu dem früheren Pförtnerhaus zu verlegen.

DOWNPATRICK RAILWAY MUSEUM

Among the companies which formerly operated major railway networks in the north of Ireland was the Belfast and County Down Railway (BCDR). From its Belfast terminus at Queen's Quay the system served, from 1848 onwards, many important fishing ports and market towns including Comber, Donaghadee, Ballynahinch, Downpatrick, Ardglass and Newcastle as well as catering for Belfast suburban traffic. Absorbed into the Ulster Transport Authority in 1948, it was clear that its days were numbered, and the entire 130 km system with the exception of the Queen's Quay to Bangor line (20 km) was closed in 1950.

In 1985 a new company, the Downpatrick and Ardglass Railway Co., was formed with the intention of re-opening a section of the line with the support of the Downpatrick Railway Society and Down District Council. The objective was achieved in 1990 when a new station was erected near the site of the original at Downpatrick and a 1.6 section of track relaid along the formation towards Newcastle with a new platform at Viking King Magnus's Grave and terminating 800m short of Ballydugan Mill.

In 2001 a further extension of the line towards Inch Abbey was opened with the rebuilding of an additional 2.8 km. This involved the refurbishment of the 52m long Quoile River Bridge with new steel girders each of 26m span. The first passenger train since the closing of the BCDR crossed the Quoile on 4 August 2001.

The railway operation, based at Downpatrick, includes a museum devoted mainly to the BCDR. The station yard itself reflects the various architectural styles of railway companies in the North of Ireland and there is an impressive signal cabin, goods shed and locomotive shed. Train rides operate using a variety of rolling stock and motive power. Steam is provided by a former Irish Sugar Company Orenstein & Koppel 0-4-0T while diesel traction is also present. The D&AR has taken delivery of a former Leyland railbus which will also be in use this season.

Location: Market Street, Downpatrick, Co. Down
Access: Inter City and local services to Lisburn or Belfast. Local transport to Downpatrick.
Operation: St. Patrick's Day, Easter Sun. & Mon,. Sat. & Sun. during July & August & first two weekends in Sept., 14.00—17.00 hrs.
Telephone: (028)—446 15779
Website: www.ukhrail.uel.ac.uk/drm/drm/html

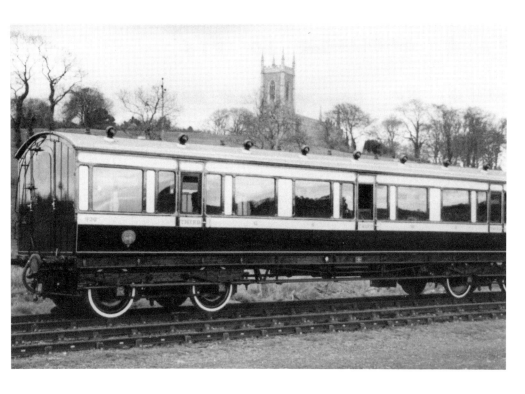

GSWR carriage no. 86 restored by Downpatrick Railway Museum
(G. Cochrane)

Parmi les compagnies qui opéraient autrefois les réseaux ferroviaires les plus importants du Nord de l'Irlande, figure le Belfast and County Down Railway (BCDR). Depuis son terminus de Queen's Quay, situé à Belfast, le réseau desservit, à partir de 1848, de nombreux grands ports de pêche et bourgs, ainsi que le trafic de la banlieue de Belfast. Absorbée par les autorités du transport de l'Ulster en 1948, il est clair que ses jours furent comptés et tout le réseau de 130 km, à l'exception de la ligne Bangor - Queen's Quay, (20 km) fut fermé en 1950.

En 1985, une nouvelle compagnie, la Downpatrick and Ardglass Railway Co., fut créée avec l'intention de ré-ouvrir une section de la ligne. Son objectif fut atteint en 1990, lorsqu'une nouvelle gare fut érigée près du site d'origine de Downpatrick et qu'une section de 1,6 km de piste fut réaménagée le long de la formation en direction de Newcastle avec une nouvelle plate-forme à Viking King Magnus's Grave (Tombeau du roi Magnus) et aboutissant à 800m de Ballydugan Mill. En 2001, une autre extension de la ligne en direction d'Inch Abbey fut ouverte avec la reconstruction de 2,8 km supplémentaires. Ceci impliqua la remise à neuf du pont de la rivière Quoile de 52 m de long, à l'aide de nouvelles poutres en acier d'un volant de 26m chacune. Le premier train de voyageurs croisa la rivière Quoile pour la première fois le 4 août 2001, depuis la fermeture du BCDR.

L'opération ferroviaire, basée à Downpatrick, comprend un musée consacré principalement à BCDR. La cour de la gare reflète à elle seule les divers styles architecturaux des compagnies de chemin de fer du Nord de l'Irlande et comprend un poste d'aiguillage, une halle à marchandises et un dépôt de locomotives impressionnants. Les trains fonctionnent en utilisant une grande variété de parcs à wagons et la force motrice. La vapeur est fournie par une ancienne compagnie irlandaise de fabrication de sucre, Orenstein & Koppel 0-2-0T alors que la traction Diesel est également présente.

Eine der Firmen, die früher wichtige Einsenbahnstrecken im Norden Irlands betrieb, war die Belfast and County Down Railway (BCDR). Von dem Endbahnhof in Belfast am Queen's Quay versorgte das System ab 1848 viele wichtige Fischereihäfen und Marktstädte und auch die Vororte Belfasts. Nach der Übernahme durch die Ulster Transport Authority im Jahre 1948 war klar, dass ihre Tage gezählt waren, und das gesamte System von 130 km Länge, mit Ausnahme der Strecke von Queen's Quay nach Bangor (20 km), wurde 1950 stillgelegt.

Im Jahre 1985 wurde eine neue Gesellschaft gegründet, die Downpatrick and Ardglass Railway Co., mit der Absicht, einen Teil der Strecke wieder in Betrieb zu nehmen. Dieses Ziel wurde 1990 erreicht, als in der Nähe des ursprünglichen Standorts Downpatrick ein neuer Bahnhof gebaut wurde und neue Gleise auf einem 1,6 km langen Streckenabschnitt in Richtung Newcastle gelegt wurden, mit einem neuen Bahnhof am Grab des Vikingerkönigs Magnus und der Endstation 800 m vor Ballydugan Mill. 2001 wurde ein weiteres Teilstück in Richtung Inch Abbey mit der Wiederherstellung von 2,8 km Strecke eröffnet. Dabei wurde u. a. die 52 m lange Quoile River Bridge mit 26 m langen Stahlträgern restauriert. Der erste Personenzug seit der Schließung der BCDR überquerte den Fluss Quoile am 4. August 2001.

Der Einsenbahnbetrieb mit der Basis in Downpatrick umfasst auch ein Museum, dass hauptsächlich der BCDR gewidmet ist. Das Gelände des Bahnhofs mit einem beeindruckenden Signalhäuschen, Güter- und Lokomotivschuppen spiegelt die unterschiedlichen Arten der Eisenbahngesellschaften im Norden Irlands wieder. Auf den Fahrstrecken werden eine Vielzahl von Waggons und Antriebsmaschinen eingesetzt. Eine Orenstein & Koppel 0-2-0T der früheren Irish Sugar Company sorgt für den Dampfantrieb, aber es gibt auch Diesellokomotiven.

FOYLE VALLEY RAILWAY MUSEUM

Four different railway systems once served the historic Derry City on the banks of the River Foyle. The London, Midland and Scottish Railway's Northern Counties Committee line connected the city with Belfast via Coleraine, terminating at Derry Waterside Station, while there were two extensive narrow gauge systems, the County Donegal Railway and the Londonderry and Lough Swilly Railway, which between them served the North West. The Great Northern Railway of Ireland came into Derry via Portadown and Strabane and its station was at Foyle Road.

The existing two-tier metal bridge linking both sides of the city across the River Foyle once boasted a dual-gauge railway link on its lower deck which connected the CDR at Victoria Road with the rest of the system for goods transfers. By 1965 all was gone save the LMS/NCC connection at Waterside, now operated by Northern Ireland Railways.

Several attempts were made to commemorate the narrow-gauge system in Derry but it was the establishment of the Foyle Valley Railway and Museum, a joint venture between a local railway enthusiasts' society and the Derry City Council, which finally succeeded. A museum and workshop centre was opened on the site of the former GNR(I) terminus at Foyle Road and 4.8 km of narrow-gauge track laid along the formation of the old Great Northern line with the intention of extending at least 10 km to and across the Border to St. Johnston, Co. Donegal.

A very interesting railway museum comprising two steam locomotives, railcars and passenger and goods vehicles from the former CDR has been assembled and is on view at the railway centre, while plans remain to re-open the narrow-gauge line already being constructed, using both steam and diesel railcars.

Location: Foyle Valley Railway Museum Centre, Foyle Road, Derry City.
Access: Inter City to Belfast, NIR service to Derry.
Operation: Closed for refurbishment for the 2002 season. *Enquires welcome.*
Telephone: 048 71 265234

Former County Donegal Railcar no. 12 at Foyle Valley Railway Museum

Quatre différents réseaux ferroviaires desservaient autrefois la ville de Derry sur les rives de la rivière Foyle. La ligne du comité des comtés du Nord du chemin de fer écossais, du centre et de Londres reliait la ville à Belfast via Coleraine, pour aboutir à la gare de Derry Waterside, alors qu'il existait deux vastes réseaux ferroviaires à voie étroite, le County Donegal Railway et le Londonderry et Lough Swilly Railway, qui desservaient, à tous les deux, le Nord-Ouest. Le réseau du Great Northern Railway of Ireland entrait dans Derry via Portadown et Strabane et sa gare était située sur Foyle Road. En 1965, tout disparut sauf la liaison LMS/NCC de Waterside desservie actuellement par Northern Ireland Railways.

Plusieurs tentatives de commémoration du réseau ferroviaire à voie étroite de Derry eurent lieu, mais ce fut l'établissement du chemin de fer de Foyle Valley et de son musée, une coentreprise fondée entre une association locale de passionnés du chemin de fer et le conseil municipal de la ville de Derry, qui finit par l'emporter. Un musée et un centre d'ateliers furent ouverts sur le site de l'ancien terminus GNR(I) situé sur Foyle Road ainsi qu'une ligne de chemin de fer à voie étroite de 1,8 km de long, située le long de la formation de l'ancienne ligne du Great Northern avec une intention d'élargissement d'au moins 10 km sur et au-delà de la frontière avec St. Johnston, dans le comté de Donegal.

Un musée du chemin de fer très intéressant présentant deux locomotives à vapeur, des autorails et des véhicules à voyageurs et à marchandises de l'ex CDR a été aménagé et ouvert sur le nœud ferroviaire, alors que la réouverture de la ligne à voie étroite déjà en cours de construction à l'aide d'autorails à vapeur et Diesel, continue d'être envisagée.

Vier verschiedene Einsenbahnsysteme versorgten einst die historische Stadt Derry an dem Ufern des Flusses Foyle. Die London-, Midland- und die Scottish Railway's Northern Counties Committee Line verbanden die Stadt via Coleraine mit Belfast. Der Endbahnhof war Derry Waterside Station, und zwei umfangreiche Schmalspursysteme, die County Donegal Railway und the Londonderry and Lough Swilly Railway, versorgten gemeinsam den Nordwesten. Die Great Northern Railway of Ireland fuhr über Portadown und Straban nach Derry – ihr Bahnhof war in der Foyle Road. Im Jahre 1965 was alles vorbei, mit Ausnahme der LMS/NCC-Verbindung in Waterside, die nun von der Northern Ireland Railway betrieben wurde.

Es wurden mehrere Versuche gemacht, dem Schmalspursystem in Derry zu gedenken, aber es war die Eröffnung der Foyle Valley Railway und des Museums, einem Gemeinschaftsunternehmen der örtlichen Gesellschaft der Eisenbahnenthusiasten und dem Derry City Council, was schließlich zum Erfolg führte. Ein Museum- und Workshop-Zentrum wurde auf dem Gelände des früheren GNR(I)-Endbahnhofs in der Foyle Road eröffnet, und eine 4,8 km lange Schmalspurstrecke wurde entlang der Gleisführung der alten Great Northern Line gelegt, mit der Absicht, dieses Strecke um mindestens 10 km bis zur Grenze und darüber hinaus nach St. Johnston in Co. Donegal zu verlängern.

Ein sehr interessantes Eisenbahnmuseum mit zwei Dampflokomotiven, Triebwagen, Güter- und Personenwaggons der früheren CDR, zusammengestellt und zur Besichtigung im Eisenbahnzentrum. Es bestehen Pläne, die Schmalspurlinie, die bereits rekonstruiert wird, mit Dampf- und Diesellokomotiven wieder in Berieb zu nehmen.

FRY MODEL RAILWAY

To catch a flavour of what it was all really like in the heyday of Irish public transport, a visit to the Fry Model Railway at Malahide Castle is a must. It was the brainchild of Dubliner Cyril Fry and his wife who began model-making in the 1920s, using as their subjects the wide and varied assortment of vehicles and styles then to be seen throughout the railway and tramway systems and bus companies of the country.

The Frys added to the collection down through the years until their suburban dormer-bungalow at Churchtown in the south of the city was almost totally taken over. Visitors from all over the world called at the house to view the marvellous re-creation of a world fast slipping away. The models are built to 'O' gauge and are in scale throughout. Many of them were fashioned from tinplate and the wheels turned on the lathe at the couple's home.

By the time they were finished — if such a project can ever be deemed at an end — the Frys had added some overseas examples for good measure, as well as faithful reproductions of familiar Dublin street scenes such as O'Connell Bridge complete with trams, ferries, barges and many superbly detailed architectural landmarks from other parts of the country.

The whole system was bequeathed to the State and reassembled at Malahide Castle. The man who was responsible for rejuvenating the collection and adding DART and other modern examples of Irish railway traction for good measure was Tommy Tighe, an accomplished engineer and model maker who also provided examples for the West Cork Model Railway Village at Clonakilty (See pps 24—27). Irish and international exhibits from the earliest railway developments are operated on a layout which includes stations, bridges, trams, buses and barges.

Location: Malahide Castle Demesne, Malahide, Co. Dublin.
Access: DART or outer suburban rail from Dublin, Dundalk and intermediate points.
Operation: April–Sept: Mon.–Sat. 10.00–17.00. Suns. & public holidays 14.00–18.00.
Telephone: 00–353–1846 3779
Email: fryrailway@dublintourism.ie
Website: www.visitdublin.com

A conspectus of Irish railway history on the Fry Model Railway

Pour avoir une idée de ce à quoi ressemblaient vraiment les heures de gloire du transport public irlandais, une visite du chemin de fer miniature de Fry au Château de Malahide s'impose. Ce fut l'idée originale de Cyril Fry, originaire de Dublin et de son épouse, qui commencèrent le modélisme dans les années 20, en utilisant comme sujets, le vaste assortiment varié de véhicules et de styles qui seront ensuite aperçus dans les réseaux ferroviaires et de tramways ainsi que dans les compagnies de bus du pays.

Au moment où ils terminèrent— si l'on peut considérer qu'un tel projet puisse être jamais achevé — les Fry décidèrent d'ajouter quelques modèles étrangers, pour faire bonne mesure, ainsi que des reproductions fidèles de scènes familières des rues de Dublin comme le pont O'Connell avec ses trams, ses ferries, ses péniches et de nombreux points d'intérêt architectural superbement détaillés, provenant d'autres régions du pays.

Toute leur réalisation fut léguée à l'état et remontée au château de Malahide. L'homme qui fut chargé de rajeunir la collection et d'ajouter des DART et d'autres modèles modernes de traction ferroviaire irlandaise, pour faire bonne mesure, fut Tommy Tighe, un ingénieur accompli et modéliste qui fournit également des modèles du village miniature du chemin de fer de West Cork de Clonakilty (Cf. pps 24—27). L'agencement des modèles des expositions irlandaises et internationales sur les tous premiers développements du chemin de fer, présente des gares, des ponts, des bus et des péniches.

Um ein Gefühl dafür zu bekommen, wie es zur Blütezeit des irischen öffentlichen Verkehrswesens wirklich war, ist der Besuch der Fry Model Railway beim Malahide Castle ein Muss. Die Idee zur Fry Model Railway stammt von dem Dubliner Cyril Fry und seiner Frau, die in den 20er Jahren mit dem Modellbau begannen und die vielen verschiedenen Fahrzeuge und Fahrzeugarten des Eisenbahn-, Straßenbahn- und Bussystems, die damals über all im Land zu sehen waren, als Vorbilder nahmen.

Als sie fertig waren – wenn ein solches Projekt jemals fertig werden kann – hatten sie auch einige Modelle aus Übersee und außerdem naturgetreue Nachbauten bekannter Dubliner Straßenszenen wie die O'Connell Bridge mit Straßenbahnen, Fähren, Lastkähnen und vielen sehr detaillierten architektonischen Wahrzeichen von anderen Teilen des Landes hinzugefügt.

Das ganze System wurde dem Staat geschenkt und am Malahide Castle aufgebaut. Der Mann, der für die Aktualisierung der Sammlung verantwortlich war und den DART und andere moderne Beispiele irischer Eisenbahnkultur hinzufügte, war Tommy Tighe, ein erfolgreicher Ingenieur und Modellbauer, der auch Stücke für die West Cork Model Railway Village in Clonakilty zur Verfügung stellte (siehe Seiten 24–27). Ausgestellt sind irische und internationale Beispiele des frühsten Einsenbahnzeitalters, u.a. Bahnhöfe, Brücken, Straßenbahnen, Busse und Lastkähne.

GIANT'S CAUSEWAY & BUSHMILLS RAILWAY

The original Giant's Causeway, Portrush & Bush Valley Railway and Tramway Company was a 12.8 km, 914mm gauge railway which opened in 1883 to become the world's first to be powered by hydro-electricity. Linking Portrush, an important seaside resort, with Bushmills, the home of the what is claimed as the world's oldest licensed distillery (1608) and the major tourist attraction of the Giant's Causeway, the line was powered by turbines located on the nearby River Bush. After initial difficulties, only to be expected with what was a virtually untried means of propulsion, the line was primarily operated by electricity, with steam locomotives being used to supplement electric traction at busy periods. Electricity took over completely during the 1920s.

The line was immensely popular with tourists as well as locals, attested to by numerous early photographic views which found their way onto postcards. However, by the mid-1930s there was increasing road competition and the railway trade dwindled, save for a reprieve during World War II. In 1949 the original company, having survived economic depressions and two world conflicts, finally succumbed to 'progress' and appealed for assistance to the notoriously anti-railway Ulster Transport Authority with the predictable consequences.

Closure came in September 1949 and it seemed truly the end of the line for this quaint and innovative little railway. For 50 years the last 3.2km of track bed remained a public footpath. With the availability of locomotives and other equipment from Lord O'Neill's Shane Castle Railway the re-use of the site for a tourist railway was proposed by David Laing, who has subsequently directed the operation.

The transfer from one part of Antrim to another saw the new venture complete with steam locomotives and superbly reproduced station buildings which echo local designs from the past. The locomotives – two steam and one diesel – have been repainted in liveries from former railway companies operating in Northern Ireland. Steam has returned again to this beautiful corner of Co. Antrim after an absence of more than 75 years!

Location: Giants Causeway, Co. Antrim, Northern Ireland
Access: Intercity rail to Belfast served from Dublin and intermediate points, Northern Ireland Railways service to Portrush, local transport. Railtours Ireland Ltd. (00–353–1–856 0045) run a daily tour from Dublin, Mon.– Sat. throughout the year excepts Suns. & public holidays.
Operation: Daily for 2 weeks at Easter; daily mid-May-end Sept., weekends at other times.
Telephone: 028–2073 2594 **Email:** info@gcbr.org.uk
Website: www.gcbr.org.uk

No. 3, "Shane" runs again on the Giant's Causeway & Bushmills Railway

La compagnie ferroviaire et de tramways originale, Giant's Causeway, Portrush & Bush Valley, possédant un chemin de fer de 12,8 km de longueur et des écartements de voie de 914 mm, ouvrit en 1883 pour devenir la première au monde à être alimentée par l'hydroélectricité. Reliant Portrush, une importante station balnéaire à Bushmills, la capitale de celle qui se revendique comme la plus ancienne distillerie patentée au monde (1608) et l'attraction touristique majeure du Giant's Causeway, la ligne était alimentée par des turbines situées aux abords de la rivière Bush.

La ligne fut immensément populaire, tant auprès des touristes que des habitants locaux. Cependant, au milieu des années 30, la concurrence des routes augmenta et en 1949, la compagnie d'origine, ayant réussi à survivre aux récessions économiques et à deux conflits mondiaux, succomba finalement au 'progrès'. Elle ferma en septembre 1949 et il sembla que ce fut vraiment la fin de la ligne pour ce petit chemin de fer singulier et innovateur. Pendant près de 50 ans, la dernière assiette de voie d'une longueur de 3,2 km servit de sentier public pour piétons. Grâce à la mise à disposition des locomotives et des autres équipements du chemin de fer du château de Lord O'Neill's Shane, la réouverture du site comme chemin de fer pour touristes fut proposée par David Laing, qui prit, par la suite, la direction des opérations.

Le transfert d'une partie d'Antrim à une autre, vit la création d'une nouvelle compagnie avec des locomotives à vapeur et des bâtiments de gare superbement reproduits qui rappellent le design local du passé. Les locomotives – deux à vapeur et une Diesel – furent repeintes dans les couleurs des anciennes compagnies ferroviaires opérant dans le Nord de l'Irlande.

Der originale Giant's Causeway, die Portrush & Bush Valley Railway and Tramway Company, war eine 12,8 km lange Eisenbahn mit einer Spur von 914mm, die 1883 als die erste hydroelektrisch angetriebene Eisenbahn der Welt eröffnet wurde. Die Eisenbahn verband Portrush, einen bedeutenden Seekurort, mit Bushmills, dem Standort der angeblich ältesten lizensierten Distille der Welt (1608) und eine der größten Touristenattraktionen des Giant's Causeway. Die Bahn erhielt ihren Strom von Turbinen, die sich an dem nahegelegenen Fluss Bush befanden.

Die Strecke war bei Touristen aber auch bei den Ortsansässigen äußerst beliebt. Mitte der 30er Jahre gab es jedoch mehr und mehr Wettbewerb durch den Straßenverkehr und 1949 erlag die ursprüngliche Gesellschaft, die die wirtschaftliche Depression und zwei Weltkriege überlebt hatte, dem „Fortschritt". Die Gesellschaft wurde im September 1949 geschlossen und es schien wirklich das Ende diese idyllischen und innovativen Eisenbahn zu sein. 50 Jahre lang wurden die letzten 3,2 km der Streckenführung als öffentlicher Fußweg genutzt. Da Lokomotiven und andere Ausrüstungen von Lord O'Neills Castle Railway zur Verfügung standen, schlug David Laing, der dann auch den Betrieb leitete, die Wiederbenutzung des Geländes als eine Touristenstrecke vor.

Durch den Transfer von einem Teil von Antrim zu einem anderen wurde das Unternehmen durch Dampflokomotiven und hervorragend nachgebildete Bahnhofsgebäude vervollständigt, die die örtlichen Baustiele der Vergangenheit zeigen. Die Lokomotiven – zwei Dampflokomotiven und eine Diesellok – wurden im Design früherer Einsenbahngesellschaften von Nordirland lackiert.

HELL'S KITCHEN RAILWAY BAR & MUSEUM

The result of one man's lifelong interest in railways and railway memorabilia, the Hell's Kitchen Railway Museum & Bar is located in the Co. Roscommon town of Castlerea and is a veritable Aladdin's Cave of railwayana, much of it more than a hundred years old. The proprietor, Seán Browne, has been travelling all over Ireland's railway system since he was a boy, and made it his life's ambition to create a museum in honour of the railway families who served the country's system through good times and bad.

Most of the collection is made up of artefacts and includes some very unusual examples such as the cast metal station nameplates from Achill, terminus of a light railway which served the western island until its closure in 1937. There are staffs, lamps, and engineering equipment from all the major railway companies together with pictures and documentation.

One of the major visitor attractions at Hell's Kitchen is locomotive A55, a Metropolitan Vickers diesel-electric, dating from 1956, which was purchased from Iarnród Éireann, minus its machinery, and moved to the premises where it was converted into a 'snug'. A new lounge has been built around the locomotive, and the overall effect suggests that it has arrived through the wall of the building!

"Hell's Kitchen" is probably the largest and most varied repository of railway heritage equipment in the country, with the exception of the Ulster Folk and Transport Museum (see pps 92–95). The collection continues to grow, with new additions year by year.

Location: Main St., Castlerea, Co. Roscommon
Access: Inter City from Dublin/Westport and intermediate points.
Operation: Normal public house hours, all year round.
Telephone: 00–353–907 20181
Website: www.hellskitchenmuseum.com
Email: seanbrowne@eircom.net

Former CIÉ locomotive A55 at Hell's Kitchen

Le résultat d'une passion de toute une vie pour les chemins de fer et les souvenirs ferroviaires, le Hell's Kitchen Railway Museum & Bar est situé dans la ville de Castlerea, dans le comté de Roscommon et constitue une véritable caverne d'Ali Baba du chemin de fer, dont la plupart des objets datent de plus d'une centaine d'années. La majeure partie de la collection est composée d'objets et comprend quelques modèles très insolites comme des plaques en métal du personnel de la gare d'Achill, qui servit autrefois de terminus d'un chemin de fer de campagne qui desservait l'Ouest de l'île jusqu'à sa fermeture en 1937.

L'une des attractions les plus intéressantes de Hell's Kitchen est sa locomotive A55, un modèle diesel-électrique de Metropolitan Vickers, datant de 1956, qui fut achetée par Iarnród Éireann, sans ses machineries, et intégra les lieux lorsqu'elle fut transformée en 'locomotive confortable'. Un nouveau salon fut construit autour de la locomotive et l'effet d'ensemble inspirent une arrivée à travers le mur du bâtiment ! « Hell's Kitchen » est probablement le dépôt d'équipement ferroviaire le plus varié du pays, à l'exception de celui du musée du transport et folklorique d'Ulster (Cf. pps 92—95). La collection continue de s'agrandir pour recueillir, d'années en années, de nouveaux objets.

Das Ergebnis des lebenslangen Interesses eines Mannes an Eisenbahnen und Einsenbahnerinnerungsstücken - Hell's Kitchen Railway Museum & Bar – befindet sich in Co. Roscommon in der Stadt Castlerea. Es ist eine Schatztruhe für Eisenbahnenthusiasten – viele Ausstellungsstücke sind über einhundert Jahre alt. Der größte Teil der Sammlung besteht aus Stücken, unter denen sich die ungewöhnlichsten Teile wie Bahnhofsnamenschilder aus Gusseisen aus Achill befinden, einem Endbahnhof einer leichten Bahn, die die Insel im Westen bis zu der Schließung der Strecke im Jahre 1937 versorgte.

Eine der Haupttouristenattraktionen des Hell's Kitchen ist Lokomotive A55, eine diesel-elektrische Lokomotive von Metropolitan Vickers aus dem Jahre 1956. Sie wurde ohne die Maschinenteile von Iarnród Éireann gekauft und an den jetzigen Standort geschafft, wo sie zu einem 'snug' umgebaut wurde. Um die Lokomotive wurde eine neue ‚Lounge' gebaut, so dass es aussieht, als ob die Lokomotive durch die Wand des Gebäudes gefahren ist. "Hell's Kitchen" ist wahrscheinlich die größte und umfassenste Sammlung von Eisenbahnrelikten in diesem Land – mit Ausnahme des Ulster Folk and Transport Museums (siehe Seiten 92—95). Die Sammlung wächst ständig durch neue Stücke, die Jahr für Jahr hinzukommen.

(Opposite) Metropolitan-Vickers 1200 hp. locomotive A3, of the same vintage as A55, passes through Co. Kildare

IRISH RAILWAY RECORD SOCIETY

Ireland's oldest and best known rail-orientated amateur group, the IRRS was formed in Dublin in 1946 by a small band of enthusiasts who were anxious to share information, prepare historical papers and ensure the preservation for posterity of artefacts, data and photographs of the railway system throughout the country. Their first meeting, chaired by the late J. Macartney Robbins (who became the first Hon. Secretary), was held in Hynes' Restaurant in Dame Street that October.

The society quickly became known not only in Ireland but throughout Europe and further afield as a reliable source of information and quality historical papers. A regular pattern of activities was established which included rail tours, often along seldom used branch lines and many due for closure, and the photography generated by these tours is frequently the only record now extant of some backwater railway stations, operations and outposts.

A duplicated typescript of railway events which first appeared in June 1947 soon developed into the widely-acclaimed learned Journal which now appears three times annually and circulates internationally to members and libraries. One of its significant achievements has been to augment the traditional interpretation of railway history with the vast resource of information and recollection held by the ordinary people who operated the system.

After years of occupying several temporary homes the IRRS finally acquired fixed accomodation in the former Goods Office adjoining Heuston Station, Dublin where a permanent library, meeting room and archive have been established. The premises contains one of the finest archives of railway material to be found anywhere, including manuscripts dating from the first railway in Ireland, more than 40,000 photographs, negatives and glass plates, books, periodicals, maps and drawings. Rail tours, within Ireland and abroad, are organised and the Society is frequently called upon to provide material for national and international publications and exhibitions.

Address: Heuston Station, Dublin 8
Meetings: Normally 2nd and 4th Thursdays of Winter months at 20:00 hrs;
Library: Open Tuesdays at 20.00—22.00, September to June except Christmas and Easter.
Membership: K. Walker, 55 Sweetmount Park, Dundrum, Dublin 14.

No. 801 "Mocha" one of the Queen class, the most powerful steam locomotives built in Ireland, at Cork while working a 1961 IRRS Tour

Le groupe de passionnés du chemin de fer le plus ancien et le plus célèbre d'Irlande, l'IRRS, fut créé à Dublin en 1946 par un petit groupe de passionnés impatients de partager des informations, de préparer des journaux à vocation historique et d'assurer la conservation pour la postérité, d'objets de chemin de fer, de données et de photographies du réseau ferroviaire de tout le pays.

L'association acquit rapidement une réputation, non seulement en Irlande, mais également à travers toute l'Europe et alla plus loin dans la recherche de sources d'informations fiables et dans l'élaboration de journaux historiques de qualité. Un programme régulier d'activités fut établi et était composé de tourisme ferroviaire, souvent organisé le long de lignes d'intérêt local rarement utilisées et dont nombre d'entre elles destinées à la fermeture, et les photos prises au cours de ces excursions constituent fréquemment les seules archives existantes aujourd'hui sur les gares, opérations et postes de certaines contrées reculées.

Le double du texte dactylographié sur les événements dans le domaine ferroviaire qui apparut pour la première fois en juin 1947 devint rapidement la base de l'élaboration d'un Journal qui paraît aujourd'hui tous les trimestres et dont la diffusion est internationale. L'une de ses réalisations les plus importantes fut d'accroître l'interprétation traditionnelle de l'histoire du chemin de fer à l'aide de vastes ressources d'information et de souvenirs des gens ordinaires qui travaillaient sur le réseau.

L'IRRS occupe l'ancien bureau des marchandises contigu à la gare de Heuston, à Dublin, où une bibliothèque, une salle de réunion et des archives permanentes ont été installées. Les archives contenues dans les locaux figurent parmi les archives les plus complètes au monde sur les équipements ferroviaires. Du tourisme ferroviaire est organisé à travers l'Irlande et à l'étranger et l'association est souvent sollicitée pour fournir des équipements lors de publications et expositions nationales et internationales.

Irlands älteste und bekannteste Eisenbahnenthusiastengruppe, die IRRS, wurde 1946 in Dublin von einer kleinen Gruppe Einsenbahnfreunde gegründet, die daran interessiert waren, Informationen zugänglich zu machen, historische Dokumente aufzuarbeiten und Bauteile, Daten und Fotografien des Einsenbahnsystem des Landes der Nachwelt zu erhalten.

Die Gesellschaft wurde schnell nicht nur in Irland, sondern in ganz Europa und darüber hinaus als zuverlässige Quelle für Informationen und hochwertige historische Dokumente berühmt. Es wurden regelmäßige Aktivitäten ins Leben gerufen, u. a. Einsenbahnfahrten, oft auf selten benutzten Strecken, von denen viele vor der Stilllegung standen. Die Fotos, die auf diesen Fahrten entstanden, sind heutzutage oft die einzigen Zeugnisse einiger entlegenen Bahnhöfe, Aktivitäten und Stationen.

Eine Abschrift von Eisenbahnereignissen, die zuerst im Juni 1947 erschien, entwickelte sich bald zu einem anerkannten Journal, das nun vierteljährlich erscheint und weltweit vertrieben wird. Eine der größten Leistungen war die Verbindung der traditionellen Interpretation der Eisenbahnvergangenheit mit den riesigen Ressourcen an Informationen und Erinnerungen der Leute, die an dem System gearbeitet haben.

Die IRRS sitzt in dem früheren Goods Office neben dem Bahnhof Heuston Station in Dublin. Dort wurden eine Bücherei, ein Versammlungsraum und ein Archiv eingerichtet. Das Gebäude beherbergt eins der besten Archive von Eisenbahnmaterial weltweit. Einsenbahnfahrten innerhalb Irlands und im Ausland werden organisiert, und die Gesellschaft wird oft gebeten, Material für nationale und internationale Veröffentlichungen und Ausstellungen zur Verfügung zu stellen.

IRISH TRACTION GROUP

The Irish Traction Group is one of the growing number of railway-orientated amateur organisations interested in preserving the more recent heritage of railway technology: diesel-electric traction and the generation of rolling stock which superseded steam but which is now itself under threat of extinction. While much effort has gone into rescuing steam locomotives from oblivion, few enthusiasts were aware that the early diesels which replaced them are now facing the same threat.

The ITG came into being in June 1989 with the object of preserving at least one example (and in some cases several) of each diesel locomotive type to operate on the Irish railway system, north and south. It was also envisaged that suitable examples would be restored to mainline operation, hauling the Group's rail tours. To date, all the main diesel locomotive types which have been operated by Iarnród Éireann and its predecessor company CIÉ are represented in the Group's collection.

Most of the membership is UK-based, many travelling long distances to board the ferry for Dún Laoghaire in order to participate in ITG events. There is a growing interest in their work among Irish-based enthusiasts, however, reflecting the generation which never experienced steam but is becoming nostalgic for the early oil-burners. It is to the modern traction enthusiast that the ITG appeals, organising tours all over the country from one of Dublin's mainline stations and usually involving several different types of diesel-electric traction at different stages of the tour.

In recent years the ITG has achieved its long-standing aim of operating special trains behind its own locomotives, while others have been loaned to the Downpatrick Railway (See Pps 40—43). Some restoration work is carried out at the group's base at Carrick-on-Suir station in Co. Tipperary but this venue is not open to the public. The group publishes a quarterly journal The Irish Mail.

Membership: Andy Carey, 24 Moor Croft, Eldwick, Bingley, West Yorkshire BD16 3DR.

Irish Traction Group "A" class locomotive no. A3R at Inchicore Works Open Day, June 1996. See p. 58 for this locomotive before being re-engined. (A.J. Marshall)

Le Irish Traction Group est l'une des nombreuses associations de passionnés du chemin de fer se consacrant à la conservation du patrimoine le plus récent de la technologie ferroviaire : La traction diesel-électrique et la construction de parcs à wagons qui supplanta la vapeur et qui est, aujourd'hui, menacée d'extinction.

Elle fut fondée en juin 1989 avec pour objet de préserver au moins un modèle de chaque type de locomotive Diesel utilisé sur le réseau ferroviaire irlandais, au Nord et au Sud. La restauration de modèles choisis fut également envisagée pour conserver le fonctionnement de la ligne principale et transporter le groupe lors de ses excursions ferroviaires. A ce jour, tous les types de locomotives Diesel utilisés par Iarnród Éireann et son prédécesseur, la compagnie CIÉ, sont représentés dans la collection du groupe.

C'est au passionné de la traction moderne que fait appel ITG, en organisant des excursions à travers tout le pays, au départ de l'une des gares principales de Dublin et impliquant généralement l'utilisation de plusieurs types différents de traction diesel-électrique au cours des différentes étapes de l'excursion. Depuis ces quelques dernières années, l'ITG a atteint son objectif de longue date consistant à utiliser des trains spéciaux derrière ses propres locomotives alors que d'autres ont été empruntés au chemin de fer de Downpatrick (Cf. pps 40—43). Des travaux de restauration sont actuellement en cours de réalisation au siège du groupe situé à la gare Carrick-on-Suir dans le comté de Tipperary mais cet événement n'est pas ouvert au public. Le groupe publie un journal trimestriel intitulé *The Irish Mail*.

Die Irish Traction Group ist eine der ständig größer werdenden Anzahl der eisenbahnorientierten Amateurorganisationen, die an der Erhaltung der jüngeren Überbleibsel der Eisenbahntechnik interessiert sind: Diesel-elektrischer Antrieb und der Generation von Waggons, die vor den Dampflokomotiven benutzt wurden, die jetzt aber vor dem Verschwinden stehen.

Sie wurde 1989 mit der Zielsetzung gegründet, von jeder Art von Diesellokomotive, die auf irischen Schienen sowohl im Norden wie auch im Süden eingesetzt wurde, mindestens ein Exemplar zu erhalten. Es war auch geplant, geeignete Exemplare betriebsbereit zu restaurieren und für die Eisenbahntouren der Gruppe einzusetzen. Die Sammlung der Gruppe enthält heute die wichtigsten Arten von Diesellokomotiven, die Iarnród Éireann und die Vorgängergesellschaft CIÉ eingesetzt haben.

Die ITG spricht den modernen Eisenbahnenthusiasten an – sie organisiert Fahrten überall im Land, ausgehend von einem der Hauptbahnhöfe in Dublin, wobei normalerweise verschiedene diesel-elektrische Lokomotiven auf verschiedenen Streckenabschnitten der Tour eingesetzt werden. In den letzten Jahren hat die ITG ihr langjähriges Ziel verwirklicht, Spezialzüge hinter ihren eigenen Lokomotiven einzusetzen. Andere wurden an die Downpatrick Railway ausgeliehen (siehe Seiten 40–43). Auf dem Gelände des Bahnhofs von Carrick-on-Suir in Tipperary, dem Standort der Gruppe, werden Restaurationsarbeiten durchgeführt, allerdings ist dieses Gelände nicht für die Öffentlichkeit geöffnet. Die Gruppe gibt eine vierteljährliches Journal heraus, *The Irish Mail*.

LARTIGUE RAILWAY

One of the most curious railway concepts ever to evolve beyond the drawing-board, the Lartigue Railway ran between Listowel in Co. Kerry and the seaside resort of Ballybunion some 16 km away. It took its name from its French engineer designer, Charles Emile Lartigue, who devised what has been accredited as the world's first monorail. It was unique in that it employed steam engines to haul passengers and freight along a trestle-type rail elevated about 1m above the ground. Roads were crossed with 'flying bridges', drawbridge type swinging sections of track. Elaborate turntables and 'switch' tables were located at each end of the line.

Lartigue looked to conventional locomotive builders to provide motive power and the UK firm of Hunslet supplied three for the opening on 5 March 1888. Each had two boilers, one on each side of the trestle rail, the train and contents being stabilised by two guide rails mounted lower down on either side of the trestle. Stories abound of the delicate art of balancing the passenger vehicles, with tales of customers of ample girth whose journey was made possible by placing a compensatory calf or sack of potatoes on the opposite side of the carriage!

The Lartigue, was, however, most remembered for its noise, a continuous rumbling and screeching as the train made its way along. In the event, the monorail, which never ran profitably, became a victim of its own idiosyncracy. When the railway systems of Ireland were amalgamated it was regarded as so unusual as not to be a railway at all, and closed to all traffic on 14 October 1924.

Happily that was not to be the end of the matter. The "One Line Railway', as it was popularly known, continued to fascinate historians, railway buffs and a wider public and became the object of a tourism project. In 1998 a centre was established adjacent to the original Lartigue Station alongside that of the former Great Southern & Western Railway at Listowel. As a result, the line lives again, with its distinctive locomotive and carriages running on 500 metres of track, and those curious turntables, switches and bridges being reconstructed for the project.

Location: Station Road, Listowel, Co. Kerry
Access: Inter City rail to Tralee with regular services from Dublin, Cork and intermediate points. Bus from Tralee to Listowel
Operation: Opening dates to be announced
Special groups by arrangement. Visitors welcome 7 days (10:30 – 18:00)
Contact: Listowel Tourist Information Centre, St. John's, The Square, Listowel

The Lartigue as it was, showing novel points arrangement.

Représentant l'un des concepts ferroviaires les plus curieux à évoluer hors des sentiers battus, le chemin de fer de Lartigue fonctionnait entre Listowel dans le comté de Kerry et la station balnéaire de Ballybunion située à quelques 16 km de là. Il tira son nom de son inventeur, Charles Emile Lartigue, un ingénieur français, qui imagina ce qui fut considéré comme le premier monorail au monde. Son caractère unique résidait dans le fait qu'il utilisait des moteurs à vapeur pour transporter les voyageurs et un rail de type chevalet élevé à environ 1 m au-dessus du sol. Les routes étaient croisées à l'aide de 'passerelles volantes', des sections oscillantes de la voie de type pont-levis. Des plaques tournantes élaborées et des plaques 'd'aiguillage' étaient situées à chaque extrémité de la ligne.

Lartigue partit à la recherche de constructeurs de locomotives traditionnels pour fournir de la force motrice et trois furent fournis pour l'ouverture, le 5 mars 1888. Chacune d'elles possédait deux chaudières, situées chacune à chaque extrémité du rail chevalet, le train et son contenu étant stabilisés par deux glissières montées un peu plus bas de chaque côté du chevalet. Les histoires sur l'art délicat de l'équilibrage des voitures de voyageurs abondent, mais c'est celui de Lartigue qui demeura le plus remarqué par son bruit. Le monorail ne fonctionna jamais de manière rentable et dut fermer à tout trafic le 14 octobre 1924.

Heureusement, ceci ne marqua pas le fin de l'histoire. Le « chemin de fer à une seule ligne », comme il était familièrement appelé, continua de fasciner les historiens, les passionnés de chemin de fer ainsi qu'un large public et devint l'objet d'un projet touristique. En 1998, un centre fut créé à côté de la gare d'origine de Lartigue le long de celle de l'ancien chemin de fer de Great Southern & Western à Listowel. Par conséquent, la ligne revit à nouveau avec sa locomotive typique et ses wagons desservant 500 mètres de voie, et ses curieuses plaques tournantes, postes d'aiguillage et passerelles ayant été reconstruits pour le projet.

Eins der ungewöhnlichsten Eisenbahnkonzepte, das jemals weiter als bis zum Zeichenbrett kam, war die Lartigue Railway zwischen Listowel in Co. Kerry und der Küstenstadt Ballybunion etwa 16 km entfernt. Der Name stammt von dem französischen Designer und Ingenieur Charles Emile Lartigue, der anerkannterweise die erste Einschienenbahn der Welt schuf. Sie war einzigartig, weil zum Ziehen der Personen- und Güterwagen Dampfmaschinen auf einer Schiene eingesetzt wurden, die etwa 1 m über dem Boden installiert war. Straßen wurden mit "fliegenden Brücken" überquert – Schienenstücke, die wie Zugbrücken funktionierten. Komplizierte Drehscheiben und "Rangier"-Scheiben befanden sich an jedem Ende der Strecke.

Lartigue wandte sich an konventionelle Lokomotivenbauer zur Lieferung der Anriebskraft. Drei Loks wurden zu der Eröffnung am 5. März 1888 geliefert. Jede hatte 2 Boiler, einen auf jeder Seite der Schiene, wobei der Zug und der Inhalt durch zwei Führungsschienen stabilisiert wurden, die weiter unten an beiden Seiten der Stützen montiert waren. Es gibt viele Geschichten, die von der Kunst des Ausbalancierens der Personenwagen berichten, aber die Lartigue ist heute hauptsächlich wegen ihres Lärms bekannt. Di Einschienenbahn war nie profitabel und wurde am 14. Oktober 1924 für allen Verkehr geschlossen.

Glücklicherweise war dies nicht das Ende der Angelegenheit. Die "One Line Railway", wie sie im Volksmund genannt wurde, fasziniert weiterhin die Historiker, Einsenbahnenthusiasten und die Öffentlichkeit und wurde zum Gegenstand eines Touristenprojekts. 1998 wurde ein Zentrum neben dem originalen Lartigue-Bahnhof eröffnet – neben dem Bahnhof der früheren Great Southern & Western Railway in Listowel. Als Ergebis lebt die Linie mit ihren unverwechselbaren Lokomotiven und Waggons wieder, die auf einer 500 m langen Schiene laufen, und deren ungewöhnliche Drehscheiben, Rangierscheiben und Brücken für dieses Projekt neu erstellt werden.

RAILWAY PRESERVATION SOCIETY OF IRELAND

The Railway Preservation Society of Ireland was founded in Northern Ireland in 1964 when steam traction was finally being phased out. By that date all regular steam services had already ceased in the Republic and the far-sighted enthusiasts who made up the fledgling RPSI established as their objective the rescuing of the few surviving locomotives, together with contemporary rolling stock, to perpetuate the great age of steam for future generations. The Society quickly grew in membership on both sides of the Border and is recognised and assisted by the mainline railway companies, Iarnród Éireann and Northern Ireland Railways.

Steam locomotives dating back to 1879 have been restored to working order and together with this fleet which includes famous express passenger classes the RPSI has returned to running order complete trains of coaches, thereby being able to offer the experience of mainline Edwardian steam travel. The help and expertise of the railway companies which the Society enjoys means that these vintage trains, typical of the period 1920 – 1950, can be seen in operation regularly and throughout the length and breadth of Ireland.

The Society is based at Whitehead, Co. Antrim, where it has major locomotive maintenance and repair facilities, and also at Mullingar, Co. Westmeath. It is an entirely voluntary organisation with charitable status in both jurisdictions. Membership is open to all comers and currently stands at around 1,000 home and overseas enthusiasts. The Society's contribution to the railway heritage has been widely recognised through grant aid from national and international bodies.

The highlight of the RPSI's annual calendar is the International Railtour, a weekend of steam from Belfast via one of Dublin's main stations to a terminus on the Iarnród Éireann network and back next day, which attracts visitors from all over the world. Together with one-day excursions operating from both Dublin and Belfast, the Society's trains carry over 5,000 passengers annually. RPSI trains are also regularly featured in films, among the more notable being 'The First Great Train Robbery', 'The Irish RM', 'Michael Collins', 'Angela's Ashes', and 'Nora'.

Membership: 148 Church Road, Newtownabbey, BT36 6HJ, Northern Ireland
Dublin Address: Ashgrove House, Kill Avenue, Dun Laoghaire, Co. Dublin
Telephone: 00–353–1–2809147
Email: rpsitrains@hotmail.com **Website:** www.rpsi-online.com

Happy scene on an RPSI tour. Preserved locomotive no. 4, built in 1947 for the LMS NCC, has recently undergone a major overhaul.

La RPSI fut créée dans la région Nord de l'Irlande en 1964 alors que la traction à vapeur était sur le point d'être progressivement éliminée. A cette époque, tous les services réguliers à vapeur avaient déjà cessé dans le pays et les passionnés clairvoyants qui créèrent un RPSI novice définirent comme objectif, le sauvetage des quelques locomotives en sursis, ainsi que du parc à wagons contemporain, afin de perpétuer la noble ère de la vapeur, pour les générations futures. L'association s'agrandit rapidement grâce à l'adhésion de nouveaux membres des deux côtés de la frontière et est reconnue et soutenue par les compagnies ferroviaires principales, Iarnród Éireann et Northern Ireland Railways.

L'association est basée à Whitehead, dans le comté d'Antrim, où sont situés ses principaux locaux de réparation et de maintenance des locomotives, ainsi qu'à Mullingar, dans le comté de Westmeath. C'est une organisation entièrement bénévole possédant le statut d'organisation de charité dans les deux juridictions. L'adhésion est ouverte à tous les nouveaux venus et s'élève aujourd'hui à environ 1 000 membres. L'événement majeur du calendrier annuel de RPSI est le International Railtour (L'excursion internationale en train), un week-end de voyage à vapeur comprenant l'aller au départ de Belfast via l'une des gares principales de Dublin à destination d'un terminus du réseau de Iarnród Éireann et le retour le jour suivant. Cette manifestation attire des visiteurs du monde entier. Les trains de RPSI sont également fréquemment utilisés pour le tournage de films.

Die RPSI wurde 1964 in Nordirland gegründet, als Dampflokomotiven aus dem Verkehr gezogen wurden. Zu diesem Zeitpunkt gab es in der Republik bereits keinen Einsatz von Dampflokomotiven mehr, und die weitsichtigen Enthusiasten, aus denen die junge RPSI bestand, setzten sich zum Ziel, die letzten Dampflokomotiven und die damaligen Züge zu retten, um das großartige Dampfzeitalter für spätere Generationen zu bewahren. Die Mitgliederzahl der Gesellschaft wuchs schnell auf beiden Seiten der Grenze, und sie ist von den großen Einsenbahngesellschaften Iarnród Éireann und Northern Ireland Railways anerkannt und wird von ihnen unterstützt.

Die Gesellschaft hat ihren Sitz in Whitehead in Co. Antrim, wo sie umfangreiche Wartungs- und Reparatureinrichtungen für Lokomotiven unterhält, aber auch in Mullingar in Co. Westmeath. Die Organisation besteht vollständig aus Freiwilligen und hat auf beiden Seiten der Grenze gemeinnützigen Status. Die Mitgliedschaft steht jedem offen – zur Zeit hat sie etwa 1.000 Mitglieder. Der jährliche Höhepunkt des Kalenders der RPSI ist die International Railtour, ein Wochenende mit Dampf von Belfast über einen der Dubliner Hauptbahnhöfe zu einem Endbahnhof des Streckennetzes von Iarnród Éireann und zurück am nächsten Tag. Diese Tour zieht Besucher aus aller Welt an. Züge der RPSI kommen auch regelmäßig in Filmen vor.

STRADBALLY RAILWAY

Based at Stradbally in Co. Laois, the Irish Steam Preservation Society Ltd. is primarily a traction engine and general road steam vehicle movement, but it does have a significant railway division. Though the Stradbally steam railway is a new development in that it was built in a location where there was no previous railway history, it features significant elements of Ireland's railway heritage.

Located in the grounds of Stradbally Hall where, by kind permission, the Cosby family also provides the venue for the Irish National Traction Engine Rally each August, the railway dates from 1967 when a short section of track, part of it tramway rail, was laid to accommodate a small 355.6 mm gauge Guinness steam engine built in 1912 by the firm of William Spence in Dublin for hauling trains of materials around the famous Brewery. In 1969 this was replaced by a 3ft gauge Andrew Barclay well-tank engine which had been acquired from Bord na Móna – BnM No.2 – where she with two sister locomotives (See pps 28–31) had worked the BnM Clonsast system in 1949/53.

BnM No. 2 was delivered to Stradbally in March 1969 and steamed for the first time at its new home in the same year. The line was re-gauged to suit this engine and the Guinness machine was taken to the nearby Steam Museum established by the ISPS. From small beginnings – about 300m. of track – the running line is now nearly 1 km long, traversing in an extended circle some of the picturesque wooded parklands of Stradbally Hall. The steam motive power is on occasions supplemented or replaced by a 1952 Ruston diesel, kindly donated by the Electricity Supply Board and by a 1936 Planet diesel.

The most intensive period of operation is the annual National Traction Engine Rally which takes place each year on the Sunday and Monday of the August holiday weekend, the first weekend of that month, when road engines arrive from all over the country. The railway also operates independently on other holiday weekends between Easter and October.

Location: Stradbally, Co. Laois
Access: Inter City to Portlaoise or Athy. Local transport to Stradbally.
Operation: Dates as shown on website. *Special groups by arrangement.*
Telephone: 00—353—0502 25444
Website: www.irishsteam.ie

BnM no. 2 on the Stradbally Railway
(Mark Merrigan)

Basé à Stradbally dans le comté de Laois, la Irish Steam Preservation Society Ltd. [L'association irlandaise de conservation des trains à vapeur) est principalement un mouvement pour les véhicules à vapeur généraux et le moteur à traction, mais elle possède un important département consacré au chemin de fer. Bien que le chemin de fer à vapeur de Stradbally soit nouveau dans le sens où il fut construit à un emplacement où aucune histoire du chemin de fer ne s'y était déroulée, il possède des traces significatives du patrimoine ferroviaire irlandais.

Situé dans le domaine de Stradbally Hall, le chemin de fer date de 1967 alors qu'une courte section de la voie, dont une partie était composée de rails de tramway, fut aménagée pour permettre le passage d'un moteur à vapeur Guinness d'un petit écartement de voie de 355 mm construit en 1912 par la société de William Spence à Dublin, pour le transport des trains de marchandises autour de la célèbre brasserie. En 1969, il fut remplacé par un moteur à réservoir-puits Andrew Barclay avec un écartement de voie de 0,91 mètre qui avait été acquis par Bord na Móna – BnM No.2 – où elle et ses deux sœurs locomotives (Cf. Pps 28–31) avaient été utilisées sur le réseau BnM en 1949/50.

BnM No. 2 fut livré à Stradbally en mars 1969 et fut dotée de la vapeur pour la première fois à son nouveau domicile, la même année. L'écartement de voie de la ligne fut réajusté pour s'adapter à ce moteur et la machine Guiness fut emmenée pour être exposée au musée le plus proche du train à vapeur. La longueur de la ligne en fonctionnement est de pratiquement 1 km de long, et parcoure les pittoresques espaces verts boisés de Stradbally Hall. La période de fonctionnement la plus chargée a lieu lors du Rally national annuel du moteur à traction qui a lieu tous les ans le premier week-end d'août, et où des moteurs routiers arrivent des quatre coins du pays. Le chemin de fer fonctionne également indépendamment pendant les autres week-ends des vacances scolaires entre Pâques et octobre.

Mit Standort Stradbally in Co. Laois ist die Irish Steam Preservation Society Ltd. primär eine Zugmaschinen- und Straßendampfmaschinenbewegung, hat aber auch eine bedeutende Eisenbahnabteilung. Obwohl die Stradbally-Dampfeisenbahn eine neue Entwicklung ist, da sie an einem Ort gebaut wurde, an dem es früher keine Eisenbahn gab, hat sie doch wichtige Elemente der irischen Einsenbahnvergangenheit.

Die Eisenbahn befinden sich auf dem Gelände der Stradbally Hall und geht auf das Jahr 1967 zurück, in dem ein kurzes Streckenstück, ein Teil davon Straßenbahnschienen, gebaut wurde, um eine kleine Guinness-Dampflokomotive mit einer Spurweite von 355mm fahren zu lassen, die 1912 von der Firma William Spence in Dublin zum Transport der Materialien in der berühmten Brauerei gebaut wurde. 1969 wurde diese durch eine Andrew Barclay-Lokomotive mit einer Spurweite von 3 Fuß ersetzt, die von Bord na Móna gekauft wurde – die BnM No.2 – die mit zwei Schwesterlokomotiven (siehe Seiten 28—31) dort 1949/50 auf dem BnM-Streckensystem eingesetzt war.

BnM No. 2 wurde im März 1969 nach Stradbally geliefert und im gleichen Jahr in ihrer neuen Heimat unter Dampf gesetzt. Die Spur der Strecke wurde verbreitert, damit diese Lokomotive eingesetzt werden konnte, und die Guinness-Lokomotive wanderte in das nahegelegene Dampfmuseum. Die Fahrstrecke ist fast 1 km lang und führt durch die malerische bewaldete Parklandschaft von Stradbally Hall. Hochbetrieb herrscht zur jährlichen National Traction Engine Rally, die jedes Jahr am ersten Wochenende im August stattfindet. Zu dieser Rally kommen Straßenmaschinen aus dem ganzen Land. Die Bahn ist auch an anderen Feiertagswochenenden zwischen Ostern und Oktober unabhängig im Einsatz.

STRAFFAN STEAM MUSEUM

Straffan Steam Museum, in a rural setting near the Co. Kildare village of the same name, is an unlikely location for the industrial giants of steam, much less the backdrop for a nostalgic and painstakingly recreated journey back in time to the genesis of the railway in Ireland. Even more surprising is the architecture which enshrines the whole: the former parish church of St. Jude, the old 'Railwayman's church', transplanted in 1988 from its original site beside Dublin's Inchicore Railway Works to the rural pastures of Kildare.

There are five areas within the museum itself, including the Power Hall where rare and unique stationary engines, such as a mill engine with rope drives built by Victor Coates & Co. of Belfast and a six pillar independent beam engine from Murphy's brewery of Cork may be seen working under live steam. There is the Richard Guinness Model Hall, wherein is charted the rise and rise of the steam age beginning with Richard Trevithick's prototype of the first four-wheeled self-propelled road vehicle or automobile. Other models are accompanied by portraits of engineering greats, men like James Watt, father of steam and of course Ireland's William Dargan, the pioneer railway contractor who built much of the early network and whose statue stands outside the National Gallery in Dublin.

A Memorabilia Gallery takes the visitor to sea and the development of early telecommunications with a collection from Captain Halpin of Great Eastern steamship fame together with sections of the transatlantic cable laid from that vessel to link Ireland and Europe with North America. This area also displays early prints of railway stations together with an interesting section on the first railways including the winding gear which was devised to haul trains up steep inclines in the days before it was discovered that locomotives could do the job themselves.

Lodge Park Heritage Centre, as the whole collection is known, also houses an interactive area which blends the rudiments of early technology with high-flying; you can build an arch from specially designed bricks, control an aeroplane at take-off, learn the basics of streamlining or transfer your energy into electricity. A computer station provides study material and questions and answers on technical subjects.

Location: Lodge Park, Straffan, Co. Kildare
Access: Arrow suburban rail to Sallins on the Dublin—Cork line.
Operation: Easter Sunday—September. *Special groups by arrangement.*
Telephone: 00—353—1627 3155 **Fax:** 00—353—627 3477
Email: info@steam-museum.ie **Website:** www.steam-museum.ie

"*Colossus*" no. 51, similar to the first locomotives built for the Dublin & Kingstown Railway, Ireland's first, in 1834.

Le musée du train à vapeur de Straffan Steam, situé dans une région rurale près du village de Kildara, situé dans le comté du même nom, est un lieu improbable de présence des géants industriels de la vapeur, mais plus ou moins la toile de fond d'un voyage nostalgique dans le passé recréé avec soin aux origines du chemin de fer irlandais. Ce qui est encore plus surprenant, c'est son architecture qui entoure l'ensemble : L'ancienne 'église du cheminot' fut transplantée en 1988 de son site d'origine pour être installée à côté du Inchicore Railway Works de Dublin.

Le musée lui-même comprend cinq zones, parmi lesquelles le Power Hall où des moteurs fixes rares et uniques peuvent sembler fonctionner à la vapeur vive. Le Richard Guiness Model Hall, où est retracée la grandeur de l'âge du chemin de fer à vapeur ayant débuté avec le prototype de Richard Trevithick du premier véhicule automoteur à quatre roues motrices. D'autres modèles sont accompagnés de grands hommes de l'ingénierie comme l'Irlandais William Dargan, l'entrepreneur pionnier de chemin de fer qui construisit une grande partie du premier réseau et dont la statue a été érigée à l'extérieur de la National Gallery de Dublin.

Une galerie de souvenirs entraîne le visiteur vers la mer et le développement des premières télécommunications, avec une collection du capitaine Halpin du navire à vapeur Great Eastern relié par des portions d'un câble transatlantique partant de ce navire pour relier l'Irlande et l'Europe avec l'Amérique du Nord. Le Lodge Park Heritage Centre, tel est le nom sous lequel est connu l'intégralité de la collection, abrite également une zone interactive. Une salle informatique fournit du matériel d'étude ainsi que des questions et réponses sur des sujets techniques.

Das Straffan Steam Museum befindet sich in einer ländlichen Gegend in der Nähe der gleichnamigen Stadt in Co. Kildare, einer ungewöhnlichen Umgebung für die Industriegiganten des Dampfes und eine exakt rekonstruierten Reise zurück zu den Ursprüngen der Eisenbahn in Irland. Umso überraschender ist die Architektur, die das ganze umgibt: die alte frühere 'Railwayman's church', die 1988 von dem Originalstandort neben den Dubliner Inchicore Railway Works dorthin verpflanzt wurde.

Im Museum selbst, einschl. der Power Hall, gibt es fünf Bereiche, in denen seltene und einzigartige stationäre Maschinen unter Dampf im Einsatz zu sehen sind. Da ist die Richard Guinness Model Hall, in der der Beginn des Dampfeisenbahnzeitalters beginnend mit dem Prototyp des ersten vierrädrigen selbstangetriebenen Straßenfahrzeugs von Richard Trevithick festgehalten ist. Andere Modelle sind von Portraits der Größen auf dem Maschinenbau begleitet — Männern wie dem Iren William Dargan, einem Eisenbahn-Pionierunternehmer, der den größten Teil der ersten Strecken baute und dessen Denkmal vor der Nationalgallerie in Dublin steht.

Eine Memorabilia Gallery nimmt den Besucher mit auf See und zeigt die Entwicklung der frühen Kommunikation mit Hilfe einer Sammlung von Kapitän Halpin des Dampfschiffs Great Eastern und Teilstücken des Transatlantikkabels, das von diesem Schiff verlegt wurde, um Irland und Europa mit Nordamerika zu verbinden. Das Lodge Park Heritage Centre, wie die Sammlung genannt wird, hat auch einen interaktiven Bereich. Eine Computerstation bietet Studienmaterial und Fragen und Antworten zu technischen Themen.

TRALEE & DINGLE RAILWAY

The Tralee & Dingle Light Railway was one of Ireland's most famous narrow-gauge lines, running from the Co. Kerry administrative capital of Tralee down through the Dingle Peninsula to the fishing village of the same name, with a short branch to Castlegregory. Steep gradients through rugged terrain gave the system a certain notoriety among railwaymen, and there was more than one runaway train! The line opened in 1891 and until the advent of the road motor vehicle did a brisk enough business.

While the famous cattle fairs at Dingle gave it a regular supply of livestock traffic throughout its entire existence, the T&D passed through some of the most spectacular scenery in Ireland and this asset enabled it to take advantage of early tourism. Although it lost its regular passenger service as far back as 1939 it had already become a magnet for the railway enthusiasts of the day and following World War II, when the only traffic left was a monthly cattle special, it became the haunt of such railway experts as James I.C. Boyd who encouraged by word of mouth a large number of fellow-travellers to photograph, record on cine camera and write about the line in its final years.

The T&D finally succumbed on 1 July 1953 after the last cattle special, complete with passenger brake van, had arrived back in Tralee; but that was not to be the end of the saga. Although lifted throughout and its locomotives either scrapped or dispersed to the Cavan & Leitrim Railway (See Pps 20–23), there was still some life in the line. Locomotive No. 5T (Hunslet, Leeds, 1892), which had been exported to the USA for preservation, was repatriated in 1986 to work on a relaid section.

The reinstalled track is 2 km long and runs from Tralee to Blennerville with 5T providing the motive power, hauling two metre-gauge coaches which originated in Spain. It operates in conjunction with a restored windmill at Blennerville which houses the history of Kerry's emigration, complete with models of ships and passenger lists.

Location: Tralee, Co. Kerry
Access: Inter City to Tralee from Dublin, Cork and intermediate points
Operation: Easter—September
Telephone: 00—353—66 27777

The Dingle (An Daingean) terminus of the T&D, with locos nos. 1T & 2T (L) which survived until final closure.
(W.A. Camwell, IRRS collection)

Le chemin de fer de campagne de Tralee & Dingle fut l'une des lignes à voie étroite les plus célèbres d'Irlande, partant de la capitale administrative du comté de Kerry, Tralee, pour aboutir au village de pêche de Dingle, en traversant la péninsule du même nom et doté d'un court embranchement à destination de Castlegregory. Des dénivellations escarpées sur un terrain irrégulier conférèrent au réseau une certaine notoriété au sein de la communauté des cheminots et où il y eut plus d'un train fou ! La ligne ouvrit en 1891. Alors que les célèbres marchés aux bestiaux de Dingle offrirent un approvisionnement régulier de trafic de bétail tout au long de son existence, la T&D traversait quelques paysages parmi les plus spectaculaires d'Irlande et cet avantage lui permit de profiter des premiers afflux touristiques. Son service régulier de transport voyageurs vit déjà ses derniers jours en 1939.

La T&D disparut finalement le 1er juillet 1953 après que le dernier convoi spécial de bétail suivi d'un wagon-frein de voyageurs soit arrivé à Tralee ; mais cela ne marqua pas la fin de l'histoire. Bien qu'ayant cessé son activité dans tout le pays et ses locomotives, mises hors service ou dispersées sur le réseau de chemin de fer de Cavan & Leitrim (Cf. Pps 20—23), la ligne conserva encore un peu de vie. La locomotive N° 5T de 1892, qui avait été exportée aux Etats-Unis à des fins de conservation, fut rapatriée en 1986 pour être utilisée à l'occasion de la réinstallation d'une section d'une voie de 2km de long, partant de Tralee à destination de Blennerville. La locomotive 5T fournit la force motrice, transportant deux voitures à écartement d'un mètre provenant d'Espagne. Elle fonctionne conjointement avec une éolienne restaurée, se trouvant à Blennerville qui est le berceau de l'histoire de l'émigration de Kerry, et présentant des modèles de navires et des listes de passagers.

Die Tralee & Dingle Light Railway war eine von Irlands berühmtesten Schmalspurbahnen. Sie fuhr von Tralee, der Verwaltungshauptstadt von Co. Kerry, über die Dingle Peninsula zum Fischereihafen des gleichen Namens – mit einem kurzen Abzweig nach Castlegregory. Hohe Steigungen bei rauem Terrain gaben der Strecke einen gewissen Ruf unter Eisenbahnern, und es gab mehr als einen Zug, der außer Kontrolle geriet! Die Strecke wurde 1891 eröffnet. Die berühmten Viehmärkte in Dingle sorgten für ausreichend Viehtransporte während des ganzen Bestehens, und die T&D fuhr durch eine der spektakulärsten Landschaften in Irland. Dadurch profitierte diese Strecke von den Anfängen des Tourismus. Die Personenbeförderung wurde bereits im Jahre 1939 eingestellt.

Die T&D wurde schließlich am 1. Juli 1953 geschlossen, nachdem der letzte Spezialviehtransport mit Passagierbremswagen in Tralee eingetroffen war. Aber das war nicht das Ende der Saga. Obwohl alle Schienen entfernt und die Lokomotiven entweder verschrottet oder der Cavan & Leitrim Railway (siehe Seiten 20–23) übergeben wurden, ist noch Leben in dieser Gesellschaft. Lokomotive Nr. 5T von 1892, die zur Erhaltung in die USA geschickt worden war, kehrte 1986 zurück und wurde auf einem neu verlegten Streckenabschnitt von 2 km Länge eingesetzt und fährt von Tralee nach Blennerville. 5T liefert die Kraft und zieht zwei Personenwagen mit einer Spurbreite von 1 Meter, die aus Spanien stammen. Sie wird im Zusammenhang mit der restaurierten Windmühle von Blennerville betrieben, in der die Vergangenheit der Auswanderung aus Kerry durch Modelle der Schiffe und Passagierlisten dargestellt ist.

TRANSPORT MUSEUM SOCIETY OF IRELAND

The Transport Museum Society of Ireland is the oldest preservation group in the country and one of the earliest of its kind to be formed anywhere in Ireland or Britain. For more than half a century its members, drawn from all walks of life, have striven to rescue all forms of road transport with particular emphasis on the tramcars of the Dublin United Tramways Company system and its successors. Unfortunately there was little support for their efforts in the post-war Ireland of the late 1940s and early 'fifties with the result that laudable attempts to secure a home for 'outmoded' but important vehicles went unrewarded, resulting in the destruction of many valuable historical artefacts.

The TMSI continued nonetheless to work towards its aims and those enlightened officials who understood the importance of their strivings made available a wide variety of vehicles which were stored in various locations around Dublin and the surrounding counties awaiting a permanent home. Among the prized items were Dublin's first double-decker bus, R1, fire-engines, lorries and a Dublin Corporation steam roller.

Despite many misfortunes along the way including an almost total absence of public funding, the continuous efforts of the Society have resulted in the preservation of more than 170 vehicles, of which sixty are normally on display at its base adjoining Howth Castle. The collection, much of it in original condition, is highly regarded internationally. In recent years a number of Dublin tramcars have been restored to an extraordinarily high standard by TMSI members.

Howth is also repository for hundreds of transport artefacts and a growing and increasingly consulted archival collection relating to general transport in Ireland. Vehicles in the society's ownership have featured in many films while the advice of expert members has been sought for authenticity in the making of documentaries and social commentaries both at home and abroad.

Address: Howth Demesne, Howth, Co. Dublin
Access: DART service to Howth
Operation: Sept—May (Saturdays, Sundays and Bank holidays) 14.00—17.00. 1 Jun—31 Aug (Monday—Saturday) 10.00—17.00. (Sundays & Bank Holidays) 14.00—17.00.
Telephone: 00353 —1—848 0831 or 00353—1—847 5623

The old tram terminus at the Martello Tower, Sandymount, Dublin, in 1925.

L'association du musée du transport irlandais est l'association se consacrant à la conservation la plus ancienne du pays et l'une des premières de son espèce à avoir créé des ramifications partout en Irlande et en Grande-Bretagne. Pendant plus d'un demi-siècle, elle s'est efforcée de sauver toutes les formes de transport routier, en se concentrant tout particulièrement sur les tramways de Dublin du réseau de la Dublin United Tramways Company et de ses successeurs. Des fonctionnaires éclairés rendirent disponibles une large variété de véhicules qui furent stockés dans divers lieux aux abords de Dublin et dans les comtés avoisinants, en attente de domicile fixe. Parmi les enjeux, figurèrent les premiers autobus à impériale de Dublin, les R1, les voitures de pompiers, les camions et un rouleau compresseur à vapeur de la Dublin Corporation.

En dépit de ses nombreux malheurs, parmi lesquels une absence pratiquement totale de financement public, les efforts continus de l'association aboutirent à la conservation de plus de 170 véhicules, parmi lesquels soixante d'entre eux sont normalement exposés sur le site contigu au château de Howth. La collection, dont la majeure partie se trouve dans son état d'origine, bénéficie d'une importante réputation à l'échelle internationale. Depuis ces dernières années, un certain nombre de tramways de Dublin a été restauré par les membres de TSI selon des normes extrêmement exigeantes. Howth est également le dépôt de centaines d'objets issus du domaine du transport et d'une collection d'archives sur le transport général en Irlande, qui s'élargit au fil du temps et est consultée de manière active.

Die Transport Museum Society of Ireland ist die älteste Erhaltungsgruppe des Landes und eine der frühsten ihrer Art, die in Irland oder Großbritannien gegründet wurde. Über ein halbes Jahrhundert hat sich diese Gruppe nun schon um die Erhaltung aller Arten von Straßentransportmaschinen bemüht, wobei der Schwerpunkt auf den Straßenbahnwagen der Dublin United Tramways Company und dessen Nachfolger liegt. Fortschrittliche Beamte stellten eine Vielzahl von Fahrzeugen zur Verfügung, die an verschiedenen Orten in der Nähe von Dublin und den umliegenden Bezirken restauriert wurden und auf ein neues Heim warten. Unter den wertvollen Stücken befinden sich Dublins erster Doppeldeckerbus, der R1, Feuerwehrfahrzeuge, Lkws, und eine Dampfwalze des Dubliner Straßenbauamtes.

Trotz vieler Nachteile, wie z. B. dem völligen Fehlen öffentlicher Zuschüsse, haben die fortlaufenden Bemühungen der Gesellschaft zu der Erhaltung von über 170 Fahrzeugen geführt, von denen 60 normalerweise auf dem Gelände neben dem Howth Castle ausgestellt sind. Die Sammlung, die zum größten Teil im Originalzustand ist, genießt international ein hohes Ansehen. In den letzten Jahren wurde von Mitgliedern der TMSI eine Reihe von Dubliner Straßenbahnwagen in außergewöhnlich hoher Qualität restauriert. Howth ist außerdem das Heim für Hunderte von Teilen aus dem Bereich Transport und einem immer häufiger zu Rate gezogenen Archiv zu Themen des Transports in Irland.

ULSTER FOLK & TRANSPORT MUSEUM

Located at Cultra, between Belfast and Bangor, Co. Down, the Museum houses by far the largest transport collection in Ireland. It embraces all transport modes on static display, with pride of place going to the large 4-6-0 express passenger locomotive No. 800 Maedhbh (pronounced "Maeve") which, with two sister engines, was built in 1939 at Dublin's Inchicore Works for the Great Southern Railway "accelerated mail trains" between the capital and Cork. As the steam era drew to a close this fine machine, the last new design ever to enter service in Ireland, was presented to the then Ulster Transport Museum in 1963. She stands now beside other standard-gauge locomotives of the Northern Counties Committee of the London Midland and Scottish Railway, the Great Northern Railway of Ireland and others.

The collection includes narrow-gauge examples from the County Donegal Railway (See pps 36—39) system and the Cavan & Leitrim Railway (see pps 20—23) and a comprehensive selection of artefacts from signalling equipment to nameplates and posters. There is also a detailed model railway and an O gauge replica of the famous Inchicore Works running shed [1846), designed by Sancton Wood, which includes the former signal tower now housing the headquarters of Iarnród Éireann's Heritage Office.

The Museum's transport collection had its genesis in a much smaller one devoted to road and rail transport in a somewhat cramped facility at Witham Street in Belfast, just off the Newtownards Road; it opened on its present site in 1993. To the far-sightedness of the original collectors must go the credit for saving much of what remains of the railway heritage, North and South. The recent addition a tram and bus hall has brought together an excellent representative collection of Belfast trams, a former Hill of Howth (Dublin) electric car and the Fintona horse tram of the GNR(I). The Museum also displays a collection of motor vehicles ranging from the earliest 'horseless carriage' to the ill-fated De Lorean gull-wing brushed aluminium sports car manufactured at Dunmurry in Belfast.

You'll need a full day to get around the transport exhibits. And you should not miss the adjoining Folk Museum where cottages, farmyards, a school, church, shops and historic houses and halls have been lovingly reconstructed following transportation from their original locations to recreate the rural world of past generations.

Location: Cultra, Co. Down, Northern Ireland
Access: Translink (Northern Ireland Railways) Belfast—Bangor line which connects with services from the main Dublin—Belfast line. Translink bus services.
Operation: Visitors welcome 7 days
Telephone/Fax: 02890—428428
Website: www.nidex.com/uftm

No. 800, "Maedhbh", now in the Ulster Folk & Transport Museum

Situé à Cultra, entre Belfast et Bangor, dans le comté de Down, le musée abrite de loin, la plus vaste collection sur le thème du transport de l'Irlande. Cette collection expose de manière permanente des modèles concernant tous les moyens de transport et sa plus grande fierté est la locomotive voyageurs express 2-3-0 n°800 Maedhbh qui, avec ses deux moteurs sœurs, fut construite en 1939 dans l'usine d'Inchicore à Dublin pour le compte de la Great Southern. Alors que l'ère de la vapeur touchait à sa fin, cette superbe machine, la dernière nouvelle réalisation jamais conçue pour fonctionner en Irlande, fut présentée au musée du transport d'Ulster d'alors, en 1963.

La collection présente des modèles à voie étroite du réseau de chemin de fer du comté de Donegal (Cf. pps 36—39) et de la Cavan & Leitrim (Cf. pps 20—23) ainsi qu'une sélection complète d'objets, du matériel de signalisation aux plaques, en passant par les affiches murales. Elle présente également un chemin de fer miniature détaillé et une réplique de chemin de fer à écartement O du célèbre dépôt de locomotives d'Inchicore Works (1846) composé de l'ancien poste d'aiguillage qui abrite aujourd'hui le siège social du bureau du patrimoine culturel d'Iarnród Éireann.

La collection du musée du transport ouvrit ses portes en 1993. Selon la perspicacité des collectionneurs d'origine, le plus important est la collecte de fonds destinée à sauver ce qui reste du patrimoine ferroviaire, au Nord et au Sud. L'ajout récent d'une halle à bus et à trams a réuni une collection représentative de trams de Belfast, un ancienne voiture électrique d'Hill of Howth (Dublin) et le tram-écurie Fintona du GNR(I). Le musée expose également une collection de véhicules automobiles.

Das Museum befindet sich in Cultra zwischen Belfast und Bangor in Co. Down und beherbergt die größte Transportsammlung Irlands. Gezeigt werden alle Arten des Transports in statischen Displays, wobei der ganze Stolz des Museums die große 2-3-0 Passagierlokomotive Nr. 800, die Maedhbh, ist, die zusammen mut zwei Schwestermodellen 1939 in den Inchicore Works der Great Southern Railway in Dublin gebaut wurde. Als das Dampfzeitalter zu Ende ging, wurde diese feine Maschine, das letzte neue Design, das je in Irland eingesetzt wurde, 1963 dem Ulster Transport Museum übergeben.

Die Sammlung umfasst Schmalspurmaschinen der Donegal Railway (siehe Seiten 36—39) und der Cavan & Leitrim Railway (siehe Seiten 20—23), außerdem viele Teile von Signalanlagen bis zu Namensschildern und Postern. Außerdem gibt es dort eine Modelleisenbahn und einen Nachbau des berühmten Inchicore-Betriebsschuppens [1846], zu dem auch der frühere Signalturm gehört, in dem sich nun das Hauptquartier des Iarnród Éireann's Heritage Office befindet.

Die Sammlung des Museums wurde 1993 der Öffentlichkeit zugänglich gemacht. Es ist der Weitsichtigkeit der ursprünglichen Sammler zu verdanken, dass so viel der Eisenbahnvergangenheit aus dem Norden und dem Süden erhalten ist. Durch die kürzlich hinzugefügte Straßenbahn- und Bushalle ist nun ein ausgezeichneter Querschnitt durch die Straßenbahnen Belfasts entstanden: gezeigt werden ein elektrisch angetriebener Hill of Howth (Dublin) Wagen und eine Fintona-Pferdestraßenbahn der GNR(I). Im Museum ist außerdem eine Sammlung an Motorfahrzeugen zu sehen.

WATERFORD & SUIR VALLEY RAILWAY

Rebuilt as a narrow gauge (914mm) line on the trackbed of the former Mallow-Waterford branch, the Waterford & Suir Valley, which is still currently under reconstruction, runs eastward from Kilmeaden for 8km following the river for much of its journey. At the time of going to press almost half of the route has been re-opened and while trains are presently diesel-hauled there are plans to introduce steam to coincide with the reopening of the entire line.

The Mallow-Waterford railway was originally constructed to the Irish standard gauge of 5ft 3in as a cross-country link between the ports of Cobh, last port of call for the ill-fated Titanic, and Rosslare via the important rail and maritime centre of Waterford. Built piecemeal by no less than eight separate companies commencing in 1849, the entire 195 km route was completed in 1906. In its heyday it saw some very heavy commercial traffic including the magnificent boat trains built by the Great Southern & Western Railway at their Inchicore, Dublin, works.

The line was, however, essentially a cross-country link and thus vulnerable to the rise of road transport. Inevitably its importance declined, mirroring the fortunes of so many others in an era of new technology. By the 1960s the writing was on the wall and the section between Mallow and Waterford closed completely on 27 March 1967. However, the development at Ballinacourty, near Dungarvan, of a plant to process magnesite from dolomite mined in Co. Kilkenny gave a 48 km section from Waterford a new lease of life and ore trains began running in April 1970. This traffic lasted for 12 years and the remainder of the line was closed on 28 July 1982.

At least one attempt was made to organise a rescue package, in recognition of the fine scenery through which it passed and with the hope of introducing a privately-operated steam tourist line similar to other successful ventures elsewhere, but the plans foundered. Then in 1997 a group of Waterford businessmen joined forces, recognising the tourism potential for a narrow-gauge steam railway over a short scenic stretch, and the Waterford & Suir Valley Railway was born.

Location: Railway Station, Kilmeaden, Co. Waterford
Access: Inter City rail to Waterford from Dublin, Rosslare, Limerick and intermediate points.
Operation: Weekends Jun.—Oct.; Christmas 'Santa Specials'.
Groups by arrangement.
Telephone: 00—353—51 872639   **Fax:** 00—353—51 6002
Email: wsvr@eircom.net   **Website:** www.wsvrailway.ie

A train on the forst stretch of the reopened line

Reconstruit comme une ligne de chemin de fer à voie étroite sur l'assiette de la voie de l'ancien embranchement de Mallow-Waterford, le Waterford & Suir Valley, qui est toujours actuellement en cours de reconstruction, part de l'est de Kilmeaden pour suivre la rivière sur 8 km pendant pratiquement tout son trajet. Au moment de la mise sous presse de ce guide, pratiquement la moitié de la route avait été réouverte et alors que les trains fonctionnent aujourd'hui au Diesel, et que l'introduction de la vapeur pour coïncider avec la réouverture de toute la ligne est envisagée.

Le chemin de fer de Mallow-Waterford fut construit à l'origine avec un écartement de voie standard à l'Irlande et servait liaison transnationale entre les ports de Cobh, dernier port d'escale de l'infortuné Titanic et de Rosslare. Avec une construction pièce par pièce réalisée par pas moins de huit compagnies différentes et commencée en 1849, toute la voie d'une longueur de 195 km fut achevée en 1906. A son heure de gloire, elle assista à un gigantesque trafic marchand. La ligne était, cependant, essentiellement une ligne transnationale et, par conséquent, vulnérable au développement du transport routier. Inévitablement, son importance déclina et dans les années 60, sa fin fut imminente et la section entre Mallow et Waterford ferma complètement le 27 mars 1967.

Au moins une tentative fut faite pour mettre en place un ensemble de mesures de sauvetage en reconnaissance des magnifiques paysages à travers qu'elle traversait, mais ces plans tombèrent à l'eau. Puis, en 1997, un groupe d'hommes d'affaires de Waterford reconnut le potentiel touristique du chemin de fer à vapeur à voie étroite sur une courte portion de paysage et donna naissance au chemin de fer de Waterford & Suir Valley.

Die Waterford & Suir Valley Eisenbahn, eine Schmalspurstrecke auf dem früheren Gleisbett der Strecke Mallow-Waterford, befindet sich noch im Bau. Sie folgt von Kilmeaden aus 8 km weit auf einem Großteil der Strecke dem Fluss Richtung Osten. Zum Zeitpunkt des Drucks dieses Führers war bereits fast die Hälfte dieser Strecke in Betrieb. Zur Zeit wird eine Diesellok benutzt, aber es wird geplant, zur Eröffnung der gesamten Strecke auf Dampf umzusteigen.

Die Eisenbahn Mallow-Waterford wurde ursprünglich mit der standardmäßigen irischen Spurweite als Landverbindung der Häfen Cobh, dem letzten Anlaufhafen der unglücklichen Titanic, und Rosslare gebaut. Der Bau begann 1849 und wurde in Schritten von nicht weniger als acht verschiedenen Firmen durchgeführt. Die ganze Strecke von insgesamt 195 km wurde 1906 fertiggestellt. Zu der Blütezeit gab es auf der Strecke einen emsigen industriellen Verkehr. Die Strecke war jedoch eine Landverbindung und somit dem Druck des aufkommenden Straßenverkehrs ausgesetzt. Die Bedeutung der Linie nahm unweigerlich ab und um 1960 standen die Zeichen an der Wand. Am 27. März 1967 wurde die Strecke vollständig stillgelegt.

Es wurde mindestens ein Versuch unternommen, in Anbetracht der schönen Landschaft, durch die diese Strecke führte, eine Rettung zu organisieren. Die Pläne schlugen allerdings fehl. Im Jahre 1997 erkannte eine Gruppe von Geschäftsleuten aus Waterford dann das touristische Potential einer Schmalspur-Dampfeisenbahnstrecke durch einen kurzen landschaftlich schönen Teil. Dies war die Geburtsstunde der Waterford & Suir Valley Railway.

WEST CLARE RAILWAY

The West Clare Railway is one of the most famous lines on the Irish system, having been immortalised by the song writer Percy French who lampooned the company for poor timekeeping, with a song entitled "Are ye right, there, Michael, are ye right?" Running from Ennis, where it connected with the broad gauge Waterford and Limerick Railway, it opened in 1887 to Miltown Malbay and finally in 1892 to Kilrush and Kilkee, with a junction at Moyasta. The total route mileage was 85 km.

The bad reputation for timekeeping was due in large measure both to the underpowered locomotives which operated the system for the first five years and the ferocity of the Atlantic gales which threatened to blow the trains off the track — and sometimes succeeded! Things, however, improved dramatically with the arrival of larger and heavier machines to haul the increasing traffic, both passenger and goods, through the testing, undulating terrain of the Clare countryside. One of these locomotives survives, in the form of No. 5c Slieve Callan, a massive 0-6-2T built by Dubs & Co. of Glasgow in 1892 and presently undergoing restoration.

There were great hopes for the future of the line amid the gloom of other railway closures in the 1950s. In 1951, CIÉ ordered four diesel railcars, similar to those in service on the County Donegal Railways, to operate all passenger trains while three years later steam was dispensed with entirely with the arrival of diesel locomotives for goods services. Nonetheless, despite modernisation and folklore, the West Clare finally closed in 1961, bringing to an end the narrow-gauge era in Ireland. Locomotive No. 5c was mounted on a plinth at Ennis Station.

Revival came in the form of a new company established in 1995 by local interests in the county. Agreement was secured to relay 3.2 km of track from Moyasta Junction towards Kilkee and Doonbeg, and a diesel locomotive and two passenger coaches were purchased from the UK. CIÉ permitted Slieve

Callan to go to Britain for rebuilding and visitor train services resumed over the section from Moyasta towards Doonbeg. The station house at Moyasta has also been restored.

Location: Moyasta Junction Station, Co. Clare
Access: Inter City and local service to Ennis from Dublin/Limerick, local transport to Moyasta.
Operation: Easter Sunday—September. *Special groups by arrangement.*
Telephone: 00—353—65 9051284

Manulla Junction, where the lines for Kilrush and Kilkee diverged
(W.A. Camwell, IRRS collection

Le chemin de fer de West Clare est l'une des lignes les plus célèbres du réseau ferroviaire irlandais, grâce à son immortalisation par le compositeur Percy French, qui lançait des satires à l'égard de la compagnie pour son non-respect des horaires dans une chanson intitulée « Are ye right, there, Michael, are ye right? ». Partant d'Ennis où elle était reliait au chemin de fer à voie large de Waterford and Limerick , elle ouvrit en 1887 à Miltown Malbay et finalement en 1892, à Kilrush et Kilkee, avec une jonction à Moyasta. La longueur totale de l'itinéraire s'élevait à 85 km

De grands espoirs furent nourris quant à l'avenir de la ligne malgré le pessimiste ambiant engendré par la fermeture d'autres chemins de fer dans les années 50. En 1951, CIÉ commanda quatre autorails Diesel pour faire fonctionner tous les trains de voyageurs alors que trois années plus tard, la vapeur était entièrement supprimée avec l'arrivée des locomotives Diesel pour le transport de marchandises. Néanmoins, malgré la modernisation et le folklore, la ligne de West Clare ferma finalement en 1961, mettant fin à l'ère de la voie étroite en Irlande. La locomotive n°5c Sileve Callan fut installée sur un socle pour être exposée à la gare d'Ennis.

Sa renaissance apparut sous la forme d'une nouvelle compagnie fondée en 1995 par des passionnés locaux du comté. Un contrat fut conclu pour relayer 3,2 km de voie entre la jonction de Moyasta et de Kilkee et Doonbeg et une locomotive Diesel et deux voitures de voyageurs furent achetées. CIÉ autorisa Slieve Callan à se rendre en Grande-Bretagne pour sa remise à neuf et les services ferroviaires touristiques, à desservir la section de Moyasta en direction de Doonbeg. Le bâtiment de gare de Moyasta fit également l'objet d'une restauration.

Die West Clare Railway ist die berühmteste Strecke des irischen Systems. Sie wurde von dem Komponisten Percy French verewigt, der in dem Lied "Are ye right, there, Michael, are ye right?" die Unpünktlichkeit der Eisenbahn besang. Die Strecke führt von Ennis, wo eine Verbindung zur Breitspurbahn der Waterford and Limerick Railway besteht, nach Miltown Malbay – dieser Abschnitt wurde 1887 eröffnet – und weiter über eine Kreuzung in Moyasta nach Kilrush und Kilkee, wobei dieser Abschnitt 1892 in Betrieb genommen wurde. Die gesamte Strecke hat eine Länge von 85 km.

Es gab große Hoffnungen für die Zukunft der Stecke, während andere Strecken in den 50er Jahren stillgelegt wurden. 1951 bestellte CIÉ vier Dieselwagen für alle Passagierzüge. Drei Jahre später wurde der Dampfbetrieb ganz eingestellt, als Diesellokomotiven für die Güterzüge eintrafen. Trotz Modernisierung und Folklore wurde die West Clare Railway 1961 schließlich doch stillgelegt. Damit fand die Schmalspurära in Irland ein Ende. Die Lokomotive Nr. 5c, Sileve Callan, wurde auf dem Bahnhof in Ennis auf einen Sockel gestellt.

Die Wiederauferstehung kam in Form einer neuen Gesellschaft, die 1995 von Ortsansässigen gegründet wurde. Es wurde vereinbart, 3,2 km Schienen von Moyasta Junction nach Kilkee und Doonbeg zu verlegen. Es wurden eine Lokomotive und zwei Personenwagen gekauft. CIÉ erlaubte, dass Slieve Callan zur Restaurierung nach Großbritannien geschickt wurde, und es wurde ein Besucherverkehr von Moyasta nach Doonbeg aufgenommen. Das Bahnhofsgebäude in Moyasta wurde ebenfalls restauriert.

LOCATION & RAILWAY ROUTE MAP

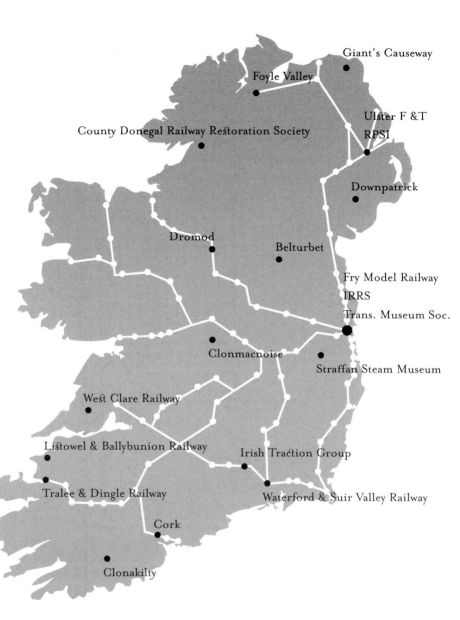

104